FROM A NOBODY TO THE DAUGHTER OF THE KING

By
Juanita Hamil

TEACH Services, Inc.
Brushton, New York

**PRINTED IN
THE UNITED STATES OF AMERICA**

World rights reserved. This book or any portion thereof may not be copied or reproduced in any form or manner whatever, except as provided by law, without the written permission of the publisher, except by a reviewer who may quote brief passages in a review.

The author assumes full responsibility for the accuracy
of all facts and quotations as cited in this book.

2008 09 10 11 12 · 5 4 3 2 1

Copyright © 2008 TEACH Services, Inc.
ISBN-13: 978-1-57258-514-0
ISBN-10: 1-57258-514-5
Library of Congress Control Number: 2008905042

Published by

TEACH Services, Inc.
www.TEACHServices.com

CONTENTS

1. The Last Fight 1
2. The Sun Shines Through 11
3. "You are Nobody" 23
4. Common Ground 35
5. Grandpa's Surprise From the Streets to Safety 41
6. A Strange Dream That Changed Everything 47
7. Falling in Love—Blue Eyes and Blonde Hair 55
8. The Meaning of the Dream Becomes Amazingly Clear 63
9. Graduation! More Surprises 73
10. A Flight to the Land of the Free 77
11. Rolling on to Other Dreams 83
12. The King Grants His Daughter's Wishes 85
13. Strange Coincidence 91
14. Thank You, America 103
15. Cassie's First Home in America 107
16. A Special Valentine for Cassie 119
17. Cassie Inducted into Alpha Beta Mu Chapter 125
18. An Extra Special Visitor 127
19. Come Let's Eat Jewish 133
20. Millet Manna 147
21. Italian Cuisine 155

Dedication

To Grandpa, the Sunshine of Cassie's life.
Thank you for the special love and care,
the twinkle in your eye,
your wit and laughter,
and that infectious smile
that you gave to Cassie for life.

FOREWORD

Most of the names in this book have been changed in order that the true story can be brought forth without any offense to any of its characters—just telling it like it was—the good, the bad, and the ugly.

The basics of the story have been told to the author by Cassie. Of course, as in most books, the author has taken the license to "paint the picture with strokes of her own brush."

As Cassie and the author remember that we are all the unique individuals we are because of the happenings of the past that we can now do nothing about, we also look forward to the future with the realization that God can make us and also those who may have mistreated us into beautiful creatures kept in His love. We pray to truly love all God's children and look forward to meeting them all in Heaven where a complete new chapter will be one of true freedom and understanding for all!

We realize that as we look forward to the future we have nothing to fear except as we forget the way God has led us in the past.

FREEDOM!

The awesome exhilaration of freedom
can only be truly felt by the caged!
The first flight of the butterfly after
crawling on its belly, reduced to its
dark existence in a tight chrysalis,
and then one day stretching its wings
to fly away to pure bliss in the blue sky,
sipping sweet nectar from fragrant flowers
—only the caged could know
the beautiful, wonderful feeling!
Cassie is like that butterfly!
She knows the feeling of true freedom!

Chapter 1

THE LAST FIGHT

She clutched her thin cotton frock close to her heart. Her small fingers nervously twisted the blue fabric dotted with peaceful, fluffy white lambs. Then suddenly she stood paralyzed with fear.

The two most important people in her life were fighting. It was not the first time they had fought—lately it seemed almost constantly that they were fighting. Things were going on that her young mind could not begin to understand.

This particular Sunday in 1977 she was only six years old but it would be a Sunday she would always remember. The big Serb, her very handsome dad with wavy black hair, was far from handsome today—his face wore a frightening grimace. As he snarled threats he was running around the dining room table chasing his much smaller Croatian wife who was just keeping out of his reach, which made him even madder.

"Daddy! Daddy! Stop, Daddy! Please don't hurt Mommy!" Cassie shrieked, her chin quivering, but her small voice choked so much until only she could hear the plea.

Mirrored in the child's brown eyes, wide with fear, was a smaller version of the bigger scene of the outside world where for thousands of years the Serbs and Croatians, as well as other groups, had fought with hard-set traditions and misunderstandings very few seemed to try to fully understand. It was just the way things were.

One happy morning in 1971 a baby girl was born—the product of two normal human beings, a man and a woman whose hearts beat with passionate love for one another. That night in their little love nest they would never have dreamed of bringing a baby into this world that would live her life in fear of being a victim of ethnic cleansing. Born to die young? What a strange thought.

As her tiny lungs filled with air for the first time, her lusty cry rang out as if to say, "I'm here. I didn't ask to come into this world, but I'm here! I can barely see, I have no teeth, I can't talk, I can't crawl, sit up, or walk. I have to rely on you for all my needs. I feel your heartbeat—the most important thing in the world for me is to know that you love me."

They named her Cassandra—meaning "helper of men." They would call her Cassie for short. She had no choice in the roles each parent's ancestors had played nor the growing hate that would mount between the groups until finally they would explode in the near future into flames of a giant war without mercy. It was to be a war of special "cleansing"—a war with numbed feelings—a war to get rid of man, woman, and child who were not of the "right" blood.

There was nothing to indicate that this beautiful baby girl with bright brown eyes and soft brown hair had blood that was any different than any other baby born on Earth. Her parents and grandparents would count each little finger and toe—she had no flaws; they would coo at her, softly kiss her tiny creamy checks and smile broadly as her cute fingers wrapped around their bigger fingers.

Little Cassie was the very first grandbaby for both sets of grandparents. The grandparents bought her pretty little dresses and shoes. She was like any ordinary baby, but of course very special to this family. But in the future she would indeed be deemed a child of mixed blood. Was Cassie doomed to die in the conflicts ahead?

Her father now tearing at the mom's clothing, gasping with sharp breaths, his fists ready to beat her in anger was met with his wife's loud screams of fear, determined to fight with tooth and nail to the best of her ability against this giant of an angry man.

"Oh, no, they're at it again!" Grandma exclaimed as she could clearly hear through the walls and down the stairs to the apartment they lived in below, "Dad, do something quick!"

Grandpa, his head throbbing from a hangover, is already running upstairs two at a time. Grandpa with a spurt of adrenaline manages to separate the two—who no doubt paused even in their present state of mind—with a bit of respect for the father as he tries to calm down his son.

Cassie now sinks to the floor in the corner as far away as possible, her arms wrapped tightly around her trembling knees, relieved by the presence of her grandfather but not knowing what to do.

Cassie's dad not only is verbally strongly berating her mom but in his anger at not reaching his wife swipes whatever is in his arms' length to the floor. Broken treasures, a sugar bowl and teapots, as well as other dishes that were on the table are smashed to smithereens.

As Cassie's mom sees these treasures which can never be replaced, some of them that had been passed on from her grandmother, now in hundreds of pieces scattered in front of her on the floor she knows that this could have been her fate, also. She had felt her husband's anger before; she would forever remember the cuts and bruises, the swollen eyes from a husband who had promised to love her through sickness and health. She had heard through the grapevine about some of his affairs with other women.

As Cassie's dad stomps down the stairs, snarling continued threats all the way, Cassie's little body jolts as he slams the door behind him

It seems that Cassie's mom already felt that very soon they would have to leave and already had two suitcases packed with little girl clothes as well as her own. Grabbing the two suitcases out of a cabinet she persuaded Grandfather to take them down to the bus station.

"I just can't take it any longer!" Cassie's mom sobs. "He doesn't really love me anymore; he is so involved with his affairs that he doesn't even listen to the needs of his wife and child. I'm sorry to have to go; I hope you understand. Maybe things will be better for your son; we just have to begin another life."

It was a hot, sticky, August day when Grandfather sadly opened the big car's door for Cassie to climb into the back seat alongside the two suitcases which were a foreboding of no return, and then opened the front door for her mom. Having seen and heard all the recent fightings that had transpired, a great sadness came over Grandfather but the matter was out of his hands.

Grandfather was an alcoholic; his overweight wife had a very, very strong personality and she let it be known many times that Cassie and her mother were not really welcome there. According to her, Cassie looked too much like her mother's family. Grandfather really didn't care that much but he and Grandmother would fight a great deal—it was common that couples in that part of the world, at that time (today women's rights are more accepted) would fight often and would usually get physical as they fought with each other.

If paternal Grandmother Bella thought Cassie was not listening well enough she would beat her. Because Cassie didn't really feel loved by anyone she would later feel that at this point in her life she was "no saint" and became rebellious. If someone would say "Go left," she would go right, because she was upset and sad living in a family where no one cared, where no one really loved her; she was so small that she really couldn't do anything to defend herself; as a result, in her attempt to try to save face and to even survive, she was not really obedient. Because of this rebellion she would often be beaten.

This was the way the troublesome years were going.

Grandmother Bella was a big negative influence as far as Cassie's self-image went. "Child, why are you eating so much! You're just getting to be a big fat slob. That's enough, you go on and play." She would never let Cassie live down the fact that she was too fat and that she shouldn't eat so much.

From a very young age Cassie would eat a lot, especially sweets. The family couldn't believe how she could eat—"it was amazing," Cassie would later say. When she was upset, angry, or frustrated, as is natural for many people with these feelings, she would eat. When she was five she could eat half of a cake all by herself. She could cover all the sad times by eating something good.

But there was a bright light in all of these troublesome, grievous years—the light was her mother's father, her grandfather Ivan who lived far, far away in a province called Bosnia. Grandfather Ivan would sometimes call on the phone.

"Let me talk to Cassie."

"My dear little Cassie, how's my baby? Are you having a good day! I miss you so much."

"Oh, Grandpa, I've waited so long to talk to you. I love you so much." She looked out of the corner of her eye and saw that her mom was already busy with something else. She lowered her voice, "Mommy is always beating me; I have bruises all over me."

"Let me talk with your mom."

"Daughter, have you been treating Cassie with good care?"

"Sometimes she gets on my nerves; but I do take good care of her."

"That's not what I'm hearing; she says she has bruises all over her where you have beat her." He begs her to treat Cassie with loving care.

"You listen to me, she gets what she deserves. You have no idea how independent she can get. You're not here to take care of her. I'll take care of her the way I know is best! The very idea of her complaining about the way she is treated—who does she think she is anyway!"

And after the phone is hung up, Cassie gets the brunt of her mom's anger for daring to say anything about her mother's punishments.

But Cassie knows how sweet her Grandpa Ivan is and that he really loves her so much; he would cry when he heard how she was treated.

When Grandpa Ivan would call, it was so special like sunshine bursting into Cassie's life through the dark clouds and all this smog. It would be something she would remember all her life; when they were talking together on the phone his voice meant so much to her and gave her hope.

How Cassie had hoped so many times before that she could leave. Her little heart sank—because she had enough of the fighting, and seeing and hearing her mother crying and sobbing from day to day, but she also loved her dad and wouldn't know until later about the deep hurts of a final separation.

The sun was beginning to burn a hole in the heavy smog—there seemed to always be smog—and things were usually very gray in this town of Nis in southeast Serbia where she was born; at that point in time it was one of the provinces of Yugoslavia. Like most of the surrounding cities there were many huge buildings, of between 20 or 40 floors high—where people lived crowded in houses that looked like little boxes.

As was very common at that time in this communistic land two or three generations would live in one house—the reason was simple, it was a matter of finances. The people couldn't really afford to live in their own houses. The families would try to separate themselves by the grandparents living on one floor and the children with their children living on the next floor. It was like a neighborhood with many such houses. Many, many people couldn't even afford a house—they would live in a huge building and have tiny box apartments.

Cassie would remember her dad, 6-foot tall, slender, and very, very handsome with dark brown eyes and very black wavy hair. There were many women after him and he really enjoyed flirting with them which resulted in a great deal of affairs. Her mom was very sad many times because of all these affairs plus the beatings she received from his hands. It was hard to be happy when he would seldom be at home with no chance to share many feelings; it seemed he didn't really care about her. Of course as time went by her dad would change in physical appearance as he gained weight, lost teeth and lost hair, but Cassie would remember him mostly as he was when he was young and very handsome. Later Cassie would remember that during the time her parents were still married she often saw her father kissing another woman and wondered who she was; this would be her dad's next wife.

Her mom was much shorter at 5-foot 4-inches; her brown eyes shaded by brown hair were often filled with tears. Her figure was neither pudgy nor too thin. She liked to visit a great deal with the people in the neighborhood. At this time in communist countries there was not much work so mostly the women would be at home, as was Cassie's mom. The women would get together, drink coffee, smoke, and gossip. Her mom would clean the house and cook, but she didn't seem to enjoy being a housewife and mother at home, this was very evident even to young Cassie.

Cassie would remember when she was three or four years old that her mother would sometimes go shopping, leaving her alone at home. It would seem hours before Mom would come home.

"Oh, Mommy! Mommy! Where are you? Have you gone away and left me for good! When are you coming back!" Cassie sobbed hysterically she was so very frightened by having to stay all by herself. She even wanted to jump out a window. Once she tried to tie sheets together with her small fingers so she could try to slide down from the second floor to the yard below so she could play.

Finally, Cassie would sob herself to sleep; if she slept maybe it wouldn't seem so long before Mommy came home again.

Because Cassie's mother was very sad so many days knowing her husband really didn't care about her, it seemed she in turn didn't really care about her daughter, either.

One day when Cassie was playing with the neighborhood children she didn't let her mother know where she was and probably just got carried away in her play.

"Cass-ie! Cass-ie! You answer me! You get home this very minute!" Her mother started calling and calling for her in exasperation and couldn't find her. Finally when she did find her, in her anger she decided she would really punish her.

"You get over here. Why did you go so far away! Don't you ever do this again!"

There was a huge cherry tree in the yard which would be full of cherries in the spring and summer. Usually it was a wonderful, happy place for eating juicy red cherries. The kids would climb from limb to limb picking the cherries fast and popping them into their mouths while the birds were fussing at them trying their best to get them first. This day her mother yanked her over to the cherry tree and started wrapping a strong rope around and around her, tighter and tighter. She tied Cassie to the tree so tight that she couldn't move.

"Let me go! Let me go! Mommy! Why are you tying me up like this? Let me go! Ouch! You're hurting me! The ropes are too tight I can hardly breathe! Oh, Mommy, why!" She sobbed and screamed with pain.

"Go ahead, scream all you want to! You're going to always remember this! Never, never do this again! You always answer me when I call—do you understand!"

Then Cassie's mom started beating Cassie all over with a heavy piece of rope. Her screams were heard by the neighbors who looked over the fences and yelled, "Stop beating her! You stop beating her! Can't you see you're so mad you're going to kill her!"

The mom was so full of rage and anger that their shouts just seemed to add fuel to the fire to show that she was in control and what she could really do to her own daughter if she felt like it; it was a terrible, unforgettable experience.

As if that was not enough punishment, the next day her mom took Cassie to the neighbors where they were drinking coffee, smoking, and gossiping. She stood Cassie in the center of the group, made her take off her clothes so the neighbors could see her blue and green bruises and berated her again for being such a bad girl, "See what a bad girl Cassie was yesterday! She'll always stay where she can answer me from now on."

Cassie shyed away from the probing eyes. She tried to cover her naked, bruised, sore little body with her arms and hands. She stared deep into her mother's eyes, trying hard to find a shred of love—trying so hard to find a meaning to this torture. Then, with downcast eyes she could not see the hurt in the ladies' eyes as they, too, automatically looked from one to another wondering why a mother would expose her child's wounds in this manner.

This was an even bigger punishment for Cassie than the beating. She couldn't at that time and still didn't in years later understand what was going on in her mother's head—something she could never forget. Her mother seemed to be so proud in her own eyes of what a good mother she was—how educated she was, etc. For several weeks Cassie's body was covered with blue and green bruises. Because of things such as this Cassie decided no one was going to tell her what she had to do.

Once when she was very small they were going to a wedding; her mom dressed her in a beautiful white dress that had been passed down from a relative's child who had outgrown it, but the dress was too small for her and was very uncomfortable.

"Ouch, Mommy, it hurts!" She pointed under her arms and to her tummy, "Oh, it hurts!"

"Now you just stop your complaining right this minute! I know what I'm doing. You ARE going to wear this dress whether you like it or not," her mother insisted, scowling at Cassie.

All through the wedding Cassie squirmed in the tight dress and tried to stretch the dress to make it bigger.

It was a rainy day and there were many little mud puddles along the road. On the way home, all of a sudden Cassie sat down in a mud puddle—she couldn't believe that in seconds the beautiful white dress was changed—what a messy child!

"Why, Cassie—you little brat! Look what you have done! I may never be able to get all the mud out of this dress! Now we have to go home and you're going to get it! You're going to really get whipped so that you won't forget it!" Yanking Cassie up by one arm her mom angrily yelled, "You just wait when you get home!"

Again she got her punishment but over and beyond the hurt, this time she remembers it as a very funny experience.

As Cassie is remembering the days in the past, her mind comes back to the reality of this day. The gray buildings and trees along the way to the bus station seemed one big blur as paternal Grandfather Earl battled with the traffic. No one seemed to be in a mood to talk; no one really knew where the next stage of the future would lead. No matter how bad each had treated the other, no matter how it could not be avoided now, there just couldn't help but be a great sadness among them all. A quick hug and a hurried good-bye was said before feelings spilled over, and Grandfather lifted the heavy suitcases onto the bus.

Now mom and daughter were on their long, long ride to Bosnia where the mom's parents lived, where the big ray of sunshine in Cassie's life lived—her beloved Grandfather Ivan! First they would have to ride from Nis to Belgrade, the capitol of Yugoslavia, and then from Belgrade to Bosnia, to a town northwest of Bosnia called Doboj (pronounced Doughboy).

Cassie stared out the window, sometimes at her reflection wondering what Grandpa Ivan would think of her when he got to see her again, but mostly at the interesting things that were happening outside the window.

Crowds of people were streaming up and down the streets, some in shopping clothes while others were dressed in business attire headed to and from their working areas. Horns were blasting a warning for other cars to get out of the way, continually being echoed by other cars' horns, "YOU watch your ownself! YOU get out of my way!"

"My stomach is growling, Mom. Aren't you hungry?" Her mom unwrapped a sandwich—a chunk of split bread with a slice of cold cut meat. Cassie ate so fast that she choked on it, then washed the sandwich down with a gulp of water from the water jar that her mom had brought along. As the bus jolted along from one pot hole to another sometimes Cassie got more of a gulp of water than she expected. When water suddenly splashed up her nose she got tickled and started to laugh but caught herself as she saw it was no laughing matter to her mother who was in deep thought.

Neon lights were flashing at cafes and bars. Cab drivers vied for customers and grew angry with each other when they got in one another's way. Buses and trucks—the kings of the road veered around cars narrowly missing them. Merchants noisily bargained their wares with customers at street booths.

Then there would be a stretch of rural areas, some with little patches of growing vegetables or grains—these little patches appearing as if they were sewn together their varied shades looking for all the world like a big patchwork quilt.

It was all too busy for the tired eyes of a six-year-old—too many things happening all at once. Finally, with the swaying of the bus Cassie rubbed her sleepy eyes and giving a big yawn fell asleep in a little heap in the big seat beside her mom. She awoke many times wondering, "Are we there!" Were they ever going to see her grandfather! But the roar of the bus and the hiss at every stop along the way as the door opened for more passengers to enter seemed to go on and on forever.

At last Cassie woke up with a start when the bus hissed at its last stop and the motor ceased. Rubbing the sleep from her eyes, Cassie exclaimed, "Are we really there, Mom!"

"Yes, we're really here." Her mother quickly brushed the last of the sandwich crumbs from Cassie's clothing, waited for the back passengers to leave the bus and guided her to the front door.

Chapter 2

THE SUN SHINES THROUGH

Cassie tried to peep between the crowded elbows tightly squeezed against her as the slow crowd of passengers wound its way down the aisle of the bus. No matter how hard she tried she just couldn't see very far ahead. She could hardly wait to see the one "sunshine" of her life. Why was everyone taking such a long time to get down the aisle!

One big grandfatherly-type man wiggled her chin, "Just where are you going in such a hurry, Young Lady?" he chided.

"Oh, I'm going to see Grandpa Ivan. I've waited to see him for a long, long time!" She looked up at him with twinkling brown eyes and the brightest smile.

"Where did you get that big smile?" He tried to look serious as he asked?

"Oh, Grandpa gave me that a long, long time ago."

The man laughed such a hearty laugh that it even made Cassie's mom forget her sadness at the time! Yes, indeed, she was Grandpa Ivan's granddaughter, that was for sure! She had his sense of humor that would help her through many difficult times in life.

"Well, I must meet this Grandpa Ivan of yours, but, first, if you are in such a hurry to see him, you go on ahead of me!" He stepped aside for Cassie and her mother to go through.

Finally, Cassie stood looking out the bus door. Right there in the front of the little group that stood outside waiting for family and friends to disembark was her very own Grandfather Ivan!

One small, tired Cassie beamed from ear to ear as she saw the long-awaited grandfather's big grin and ran into his open arms.

"Oh, Grandpa, is it really you! I've waited so long to see you again. I love you, Grandpa!" Cassie felt so safe, so at home at last! Her sunshine came in a small package—he was a very short man, about 5 feet 4 inches tall but he was very muscular; he had worked very, very hard all his life beginning with the work he did with his parents. He was a bit chubby but not overweight.

Grandpa picked Cassie up and swung her around and around. As he swung her around she saw the older man who had let her get around him so she could see her own grandfather; he was smiling from ear to ear. He wouldn't dare interrupt this special reunion!

Grandfather's wide grin displayed a big space between his two front teeth, this would also be the mark of Cassie, which just made the happy grin even more special. She would always remember that beautiful, beautiful smile. Everyone knew him for that smile; he always loved to joke a great deal and everyone loved to be around him. Cassie was also laughing when she was around him; he had the knack to be able to make something funny out of nothing.

Grandpa Ivan was a man with a big heart. What a bright light he was in Cassie's life! On the other side he was a moderately strict man who had spent a few years in the military; of course the military discipline became a part of his life.

Her grandmother was taller than her grandfather. In her younger years she always had her hair in a perm but as she grew older she grew her hair very, very long, almost to her seat. At night she would let her hair down and brush it many times, counting the strokes to make sure she did it the right amount of times to make it nice and shiny—then in the early morning she would brush her hair again and wind it up tight in a bun.

"Grandma, can I brush your hair?" It always fascinated Cassie to see her grandma's long hair and she would "itch" to brush it, too.

"No, no, Child!" Grandma talked around the hair pins tucked between her teeth. She couldn't bear to have anyone else brush her hair.

Now as Cassie's mom and her grandmother walked ahead they talked sadly about the breakup but Cassie's mom declared that it was final, that she couldn't take it any longer and that if they stayed together her husband might really do something bad to hurt her even worse than before. They talked fast, trying to get in all that they had missed from not seeing each other in quite awhile.

Cassie skipped along feeling great happiness and safety, her small hand held by Grandfather's big hand as they went to Grandfather's car.

The grandparents were sad that things didn't work out for their daughter's marriage. They tried to help out in anyway they could. They kept very busy with a business they owned—they were producing sweaters; there were all kinds of sweaters—pullovers, turtlenecks, etc., many different colors for men, women, and children. There were different cards to weave a variety of designs. Then the knitted material would be spread out on tables. A pattern would be placed on the fabric and cut out with scissors. Then the sleeves and other parts were sewn together.

For some religious young people it was very difficult to follow their convictions and go to public school. Instead of continuing on in school these young people would try to learn a trade. Cassie's grandparents always had many young people coming to their sweater business to learn a trade and then go back to their own homes and open their own businesses. So these young people would stay one, two, or three years and were more or less like a part of the family. While they worked in the sweater shop they also would help with the household cleaning, cooking, and babysitting for other workers' children. So the house was always fairly full and everybody was very, very, very busy.

Because everybody was so busy Cassie tried to stay out of the way and to do activities that she could do by herself. She really didn't have many friends. But there was one passion she had at an early age—books were her friends.

Until she learned to read for herself she loved to look at the pictures and she would memorize the pages that someone else would read to her from these books. Then as she went to school and learned to read for herself she really loved to read books. Of course if you read books you had to be by yourself. Books were always very important to Cassie.

One of the books Cassie really loved to read was about a bear. This was a story for kids. This bear had a younger friend and they ran around together trying to steal food from campers. Cassie was so impressed with the story of the bears in Yellowstone National Park and she loved the ranger's hat and coat. As she read the book she was dreaming that some time in her life she would love to be in that country and in the national park where this bear lived.

Another story she really liked happened in North Carolina and again she was dreaming of how wonderful it would be to see those places she read about. But at that point they were only dreams; she could never believe that ever, ever in her life she would be able to see the place where the bear lived and was stealing all the food from the tourists. Life is so full of surprises.

Martin Luther King made such a great impression on this little girl far across the ocean in the middle of Bosnia. To her he was saying that the most important thing was to have a dream and if you have a dream everything is possible.

As Cassie curled up on the sofa looking through a book she sometimes would get a faraway look on her face and say to herself, "Oh, if only I could go to that place it would be so wonderful!" It was hard for Cassie to put down her books even when she was called for another one of her passions—eating!

Cassie's mom could have worked with her grandparents also, but the problem was that her mom smoked and drank; the grandparents didn't smoke and drink and they had very good reputations and were well-known in this small town where everyone knew about everyone else. Very soon after their arrival home Cassie's mom started going out and meeting this man and that man. Grandfather Ivan just couldn't see his daughter almost ruining his reputation by going to nightclubs; for him this was really shame so he and his daughter were starting to fight.

One night in the wee hours of the morning when his daughter came home with a boyfriend, laughing loudly and singing to the top of her lungs, stumbling around to find the steps up the stairs Grandpa had had enough!

The next morning he let it be known in no uncertain terms that he couldn't put up with this in his house anymore. "Daughter, you made such a scene last night when you came home drunk, awaking all the neighborhood. I just can't have you doing this way and staying at our house any more! The neighbors were peeping out their windows and Grandma and I felt like crawling in a hole! It looks like even though you don't choose to make a better life for yourself that at least you would think of your mother and father's reputations and live the right kind of life around our house!

"And what about your child? Do you want Cassie to grow up living a sinful life, drinking and carousing with every man that comes her way? Why can't you think of her life and give her the very best example to live by! We just don't understand what has gotten into you—have you no sense of shame?"

"I'm a grown woman, Dad, I can do what I want to with my own life! I'm tired of being preached to. I see that I can't live with you any longer and I will find myself an apartment on my own."

After some time with her own thoughts, she packed her things and asked, "Mom and Dad would you consider keeping Cassie just until I can make some money enough to be able to keep her myself?"

It was a way out; she had no intention of having a young child to live with her and her boyfriends. She just wanted to be free, unrestrained by having to keep track of a child and "to train her up the way she should go."

"Of course, we wouldn't want it any other way; you are in no condition to take care of Cassie. You still have choices that don't include her. Cassie will always have a home. She can stay with us just as long as she wants to. She's Grandpa's precious Cassie and I won't stand to see her hurt any more. I can see that you're on the road to ruining your life—you don't need to ruin Cassie's life, too. We will always love you and pray that things will get better for you!"

The morning that Cassie's mom decided to leave to find her own apartment she took Cassie on her lap and said, "Mommy is going to another city. I'm going to make some money so you can come to live with me. For now you will stay with Grandma and Grandpa."

Cassie didn't worry; she loved being at Grandpa's house and, after all, her mom said it would only be long enough for her to make some money. This was always the excuse that was made—"just until I make enough money."

The daughter had resolved that she didn't want to stay any longer with her parents. She wanted to live her life without any restrictions by anyone else. She put on a big smile for Cassie, gave her a little squeeze, "Now you remember—Mommy's making some money so you can come to live with me." She left Cassie with her grandparents believing that soon she would be with her mother again.

While Cassie's mom chose to live in the city of Sarajevo which was the capital of Bosnia, soon she would be seen in the bars—the type of young woman who would party not just to laugh and joke on the sidelines, but she'd be the one to jump up in the middle of the table, pull up her skirts and put on a show.

As the days grew longer and longer and still her mother hadn't "made enough money," Cassie began to wonder if her mom had really told her the truth and if her mom really loved her. Many long days and many long nights it was sad for Cassie knowing that her mother was willing to go off and leave her with her grandparents instead of taking her with her. She wondered why she wasn't welcome to live with her own mom but when Grandpa would see Cassie sitting with a far away look in her eyes he would make something funny happen and get Cassie to laugh along with him.

Finally, the day would come when Grandma's helpers would get up a bit earlier to make a special breakfast for Cassie.

"Today is your very first day of school, Cassie!" Grandpa gave her a big hug and a big smile. "You're going to have fun in school. You can learn to read your very own books! You can color pretty pictures. You can make special friends!"

Cassie stroked her new scarf that Grandma had folded just right and tied over her head. She even had a new dress and new shoes; and what a lucky girl she was to have new sweaters from her grandparents' own sweater shop!

Cassie was excited to think of learning to read, but as she walked up to the big school door she was a bit apprehensive as to what she was supposed to do and as to where she was supposed to go. Soon a teacher came to show her and the other first graders where their room was. Some of the kids on their first day of school cried, but Cassie tried to be brave. She didn't want anyone to see her tears. She noticed that the other kids had moms and/or dads that brought them to their very first day of school and she felt left out! She wanted to go hide in Grandpa's big arms but she wanted to make him happy with her being brave.

It helped to forget some of her sadness by starting to school and to be among young people her age. She would try and try to learn her alphabet. Some kids already knew the alphabet; their parents had taught them the alphabet at home. But Cassie hadn't had any help learning it at home and she would cry because she couldn't learn it fast enough. Besides at that time three separate languages were spoken in Yugoslavia—Serbo-Croatian, Slovenian, and Mace-donian. These languages were similar to each other, but each language had several dialects. There were two different alphabets. It was natural that Cassie didn't pick the alphabet up quickly—after all her father wrote with the Cyrillic alphabet and her mom wrote with the Roman alphabet and each of them spoke with languages that had their own distinctive qualities. Besides that, the break-up of her family caused scars that were not easy to heal. It was not easy to concentrate on school subjects when there was all this unrest wondering why you weren't really loved, why you couldn't live with your own mother.

Still there were things that were fun in school that helped to ease her mind. At recess they would play games with these stretchy ropes that were like elastic. Someone would hold the ends and the kids would step through the strands, making different designs.

Cassie attended the first, second, and third grades in Doboj. Even though there were some things in school that were fun, at home it was rather difficult. There were arguments about who was going to buy what for Cassie—her mom and dad, or her grandmother and grandfather on her father's side, or the grandparents on her mother's side. Cassie couldn't understand at this point what all of this was about. But more and more her grandmother became really upset about the behavior of Cassie's father. She had so much anger against him, especially after the divorce, and for some reason even though Cassie actually looked like Grandpa Ivan, Grandma would always say something about how Cassie looked and acted like her father.

Many times Grandma would say, "Don't put your legs like that, you look like your dad," or "Don't lie down like that, you look just like your dad. We don't want to see that."

Cassie wasn't even aware that she was doing anything like her father did but she could see that she was doing so many things that reminded her grandmother of her father or that she just had trouble with her being there because she did remind her of her father. She was very sad about that and knew that her grandmother didn't really accept her and really didn't want her.

Sometimes Grandpa would wonder where Cassie had gone and find her in some little corner sobbing, "Why does Grandma stay so mad at my dad? He's not here anymore but Grandma always thinks I act like him. Do I really act like him, Grandpa? I don't feel like I'm acting like him or looking like him."

"Dear, Child, it hurts me to hear your grandma talk this way. I can't really understand how she can say these things to you and about you that she does. It seems she would care more about making you feel comfortable than about complaining about you even to your face, but we just have to try to love her and care for her in spite of the way she's acting.

"Things are tough, not about you, but trying to make a descent living, feeling hurt about the way our daughter is acting—wishing she would live right. Besides Grandma feels great anger about your dad, the way he treated your mom—the way he was always running around with other women and not being faithful to your mom.

"You might not be able to understand now, Cassie, but everything we do or say each day makes a certain impression on another person and they pass it on to another person until finally it's like one bad apple in the middle of a bushel of good apples. The bad apple gets a bruise. The bruise turns into a big rotten spot. The rotten spot not only eats that apple away but it makes a rotten spot on all the apples that touch the rotten apple. But you see, that's because the apples can't get out of the bag. We have to take the apples out and spread them so they don't touch each other—that way the bad apple only hurts itself." Grandpa realized that he was talking way above Cassie's head—he laughed and lightly pinched her apple-pink cheek, "You're a good apple, Cassie; try to always be a GOOD apple!"

Cassie looked up into his sparkling eyes and smiling face. It was infectious. She had to smile, "You're a GOOD apple, too, Grandpa!" Cassie's smile turned into a big laugh. They both laughed together. It was so easy to talk to Grandpa Ivan! He always turned rain into sunshine!

On the other hand Grandpa's laugh didn't seem to reach her grandmother who would openly say so many times that she hoped Cassie would go and live with her mom or her dad. She "already had enough troubles."

Cassie knew she was not welcome at her other grandparents because they felt she looked and acted so much like her mother's side of the family. And now this grandmother thought she looked and acted too much like her father's side of the family. So Cassie was between a "rock and a hard place." But again the bright spot was Grandfather Ivan; he was totally against her leaving and against the opinions of her grandmother, so they would fight many, many times together even in front of Cassie.

Cassie's grandparents had another daughter who left at the very young age of sixteen to go to Austria where she went to school, met and married an Austrian guy. They had two kids. And of course her aunt was the favorite of her grandmother and of course her kids were the favorites. They would visit once a year coming in the summer; they had everything. They were treated like angels and Cassie was so-o-o jealous. She couldn't help but notice that when these two cousins came that Grandma would go out of her way to do special things for these cousins, like buying fruit, for instance, that they would never have been able to have on an ordinary day. Cassie was always saying she would like to be treated like this—they were something really special.

"Grandma, why can't we have these nice fruits any other time? Why do we have to wait until the cousins come before we can have these good things to eat?"

She was told by her grandmother, "Yeah. You are here all the time but they are the guests; they come just once a year so they have to be treated special." At that point Cassie kept repeating to herself, "They live so far away—I hope and I pray that very soon I can live so far away that when I come to visit I can be treated special."

In later years Cassie would try to think of some positive things about her grandmother—some special things her grandmother did. Before Cassie learned to read, her grandmother would tell her different stories—not every day but almost every day. Before she would go to bed her grandmother would tell these stories. They were generally secular children's stories that Grandmother was told when she was a child and also Bible stories. At that point in Yugoslavia you didn't really have Bibles for children with pictures. It was just a regular Bible and Grandma had actually to try to modify the Bible stories for Cassie's age. This would be something that Cassie would really appreciate as the years went by. Cassie would later think it was probably like a huge battle inside her grandmother; on one side was this anger against her father and yet she truly wanted to be a Christian.

There was another important thing she really appreciated about her grandmother—because of the trauma that Cassie had gone through since the day they left the place where her parents lived and went to her grandparents home, she started to wet the bed. This happened for many years until she was about eleven years old. She really didn't have any control and would wet the bed almost every single night. It was really difficult for her and everybody else. It was embarrassing to have to have special pads on her bed and to have to have her grandmother wash extra bedding. They would try everything they could think of—no drinking of water after a certain time of day, or going to the bathroom before she would go to bed, but nothing seemed to help.

A special thing that she remembered was that her grandmother took her to a doctor and he said probably it was nothing physical but that it was because of a lot of trauma and that they would just hope with time that it would go away. Cassie knew this was very hard on her grandmother but her grandmother never screamed at her and didn't punish her for all this trouble—for this Cassie would look back with deep gratefulness to her grandmother.

Cassie would never forget one day when all of them were downstairs in the sweater factory where they were working when suddenly her grandmother said a startling thing to her grandfather, for some reason Cassie would always wonder why—what had she said or done to provoke this? But suddenly her grandmother declared, "Either she is leaving or I am going to leave."

Cassie ran up the stairs far away from the stares of everyone. Wow! It was like a thunderbolt out of the sky!

"Grandpa, I really want to go to live with my own mother," Cassie finally said one day.

Grandpa and Cassie had already talked about the way her grandma was talking to her. Now, even in her young mind she could see that she would only cause problems between her grandma and grandpa if she said any more. It was hard not being able to talk to someone about her deep hurts. But from that point Cassie decided she wanted to go to live with her mother. Her grandparents didn't really feel that this was the thing for her to do but even at an early age if she decided she wanted to do something

Cassie would try to reach that goal. The wheels started turning in Cassie's mind. She wanted so badly to go live with her mom that she would figure out a means to get her way.

"I've already raised my two girls—now it's time they raised their own kids—I'm too old to take it anymore," complained Grandmother.

"Now, Dear, why on earth do you talk like that! Aren't you glad they had our precious Cassie? She's no big problem. We can give her the things she needs; you know her mom is not settling down for any life to be a good mother for Cassie at this time!"

"You go ahead, think the way you want to------" Grandma stalked away.

For Grandfather Ivan there was no way Cassie was going to go live with her mother in the conditions she was living in, and even her grandmother, after she really thought it through, didn't feel this was the thing for Cassie to do.

"Okay, you just wait and see—if I don't get to go live with my mom I just won't study. If I fail maybe just maybe you'll let me go to live with my mom!" Cassie could see that her grandparents didn't think she should go to live with her mother and she really wanted to; she decided she wouldn't study any more for school and if they didn't let her go she would fail that year. Of course in the midterm she failed and they realized she was really serious; they were really worried and promised, "Okay, just start to study again and then you can go to live with your mother." Both Grandma and Grandpa knew how much they loved their own children and they could feel how sad it must be to be separated from her own mom. So of course Cassie started to study again and passed that year.

It was another August day, at the end of August, that Cassie's belongings were packed up and Grandpa sorrowfully took Cassie to Sarajevo to live with her mother.

"Dear, Child, you know how badly it hurts me to have you go to live with your mom, but it seems there is nothing more that I can do or say to make you understand. I know how much it means to you to live with your mom. I guess you will just have to see for yourself how it really is. How well he knew that school sometimes was the experience of hard knocks.

Even though Cassie was still a small child she was living up to her name; she would be strong and she would help others. She loved her grandfather and she knew he loved her but she didn't want to be the cause of the splitting up of her grandparents so she would at least help her dear grandpa to keep his home with his wife. Besides, she had this strong desire for her mother's love. She wanted to live with her very own mother. She couldn't believe that her mother really didn't love her enough to want her to stay with her. After all, her mom had said when she got money enough that Cassie could come live with her. Cassie didn't know that no matter how much her mom would make, it still wouldn't be enough to have her child come live with her. For her mom it was good enough to have her mom and dad give a good supportive home for their granddaughter.

"Oh, dear, if Cassie is to live with me I'll need more money than I'm making to take care of her! I just don't see how I can keep her."

"Okay, Daughter, I won't see my granddaughter going without the things she needs. We'll do the best we can to help you with her needs," sighed Grandpa.

As Cassie journeyed again to a new home she had no idea, at her age, that this would be the beginning of a very bad time in her life.

As Grandpa stepped into the place Cassie would be calling home he could already see big problems; this was no place for his dear grandchild.

"Cassie, my dear Cassie, you be a GOOD apple! Remember, you can always come home to live with Grandpa."

Grandpa Ivan left Cassie at her mom's apartment with a big hug, and a promise that he would call to see how all was going. He gave her a big smile and then hurried away before she could see the big tears in his eyes and feel his heart sinking.

There would be no easy rest for Grandpa Ivan but all he could do was to leave all in God's hands.

Chapter 3
"YOU ARE NOBODY!"

Yugoslavia, meaning, "Land of the South Slavs," covered an area a bit larger than the state of Wyoming but it had more than 60 times as many people living within its boundaries than Wyoming. So, almost everywhere one would go there were always crowds of people.

The people were needy so they would rent a room to you and you could use their kitchen and their bathroom. It's a totally different world than in other countries where it's not common that the renters would share a bathroom or kitchen with the whole landlord family. Sometimes you would be friends with this family but not routinely; most often you would someway be separated and really wouldn't be a part of the family. Usually these people needed money and you needed a place to stay so you would try to get along as best you could.

When Cassie went to live with her mother in the capital city of Sarajevo, her mother rented one such room; there were two beds in a single room with a table in the middle of the room. Cassie's mom and her boyfriend would sleep in one bed on one side of the room while Cassie would sleep in the other bed.

Sometimes there was a lot of whispering going on between Cassie's mom and her boyfriend—so many secrets. Where did Cassie fit in?

Naturally Cassie felt very uncomfortable with this strange guy she really didn't know sleeping in the room. But if she would express her feelings her mom would quickly inform her, "You are NOBODY and you are not going to tell me what I'm going to do!" She was always very, very verbally abusive and so Cassie just knew she had to tolerate this predicament and didn't have a chance.

Increasingly Cassie could see that her mom didn't appreciate her staying there. By the time Cassie became a teenager she loved her books and doing things by herself at home, like a "home mouse," she would say, but one day her mom would ask, "Everybody's going to the discos, etc., etc., why don't you go there? Why are you staying at home all the time?" It was strictly a selfish thing to say? What did she think Cassie would do wandering around on the streets, finding "friends" among kids she didn't know the foggiest thing about!

Cassie could see that her mom was not really concerned about Cassie socializing with other young people but she just wanted to have the house empty for her boyfriend and herself. After this, Cassie would feel that she just had to get out in the streets and so she started to get acquainted with other young people there.

Cassie was a very pretty, sweet girl. Anyone would want to start a friendship with her, but she was reticent about getting "close" to people she knew nothing about.

These other young people with no or little supervision were of course not the best kind of young people. They were not staying at home and studying; they would smoke and drink alcohol. It was not like it is in the States where if you would go to the store and try to buy cigarettes you would not be allowed to buy them if you were under a certain age. Here everybody could buy cigarettes, "even a toddler or infant" could buy them. You could go buy alcohol on the shelves and there were no restrictions like it is in the States. Cassie hated it and really didn't enjoy at all being with these young people but she just didn't know what to do so she became a part of the crowd—drinking coffee and alcoholic drinks, smoking, and mixing in their kind of "fun"—a "good apple" rubbing shoulders with the rotten apples.

Of course these young people didn't have that much money so it was very common for this kind of young people to beg for money. Usually you had to stand where the people buy newspapers, and Cassie would plead, "Can you give me a few coins?" She would look up at them with sad eyes and if she begged long enough then she could get quite a lot of money to buy cigarettes, coffee, and alcohol, or go to the movies.

It was hard for Cassie to get used to begging for money. She watched her "friends" begging; they told her each step to take. Her "friends" were her teachers on the street.

Of course if you spent your time that way and you didn't spend time studying, then, unless you were smart and had a photographic memory you couldn't survive in school. Instead, generally grades would drop down. There was also a lot of abuse in the public schools. There weren't any private schools in the communist reign—everything was public. There were young students who were especially strong and they would try to find weak students. They would beat them after school.

Cassie was one of those victims. The strong ones would wait for the weak ones and would beat them totally; it was really terrible. Cassie would finally not know what to do because nothing happened to change this situation. Nobody from the school staff seemed to care that much about such violence. They would just tell you, "Maybe your parents can just come and pick you up," and of course if the parents didn't come then you went by yourself, so what could Cassie do? She had to try to think of some way on her own to try to survive. Almost every single day after school she would lock herself in the bathroom and wait there at least an hour until she thought that hopefully the students were gone and then she would try to sneak out of the school and go home.

These were really sad memories because the other parents would come and the other young people were safe but Cassie just had to spend at least an hour in the bathroom. How tired she got just staring at the bare walls and smelling the bathroom smells. On the other side at the same time she was in this click, or gang, and became a worse and worse student. Not only did her grades get worse and worse but she would start to skip school because she was not prepared to take the test, or for some other reason.

One day after seeing that Cassie had missed so many hours the school psychologist called her mother. Cassie's mother was not in touch with the school. She never checked in to see how her daughter was doing. It was with some reluctance that her mom went to see the psychologist.

"Do you have any idea that Cassie has been skipping school and missing her tests? She seems to be such a sweet girl but her friends are getting her into trouble. You must talk to Cassie and let her know that you know she is not coming to school regularly and you know about her grades going down. You must keep better track of your daughter. She's wasting our time and hers, too."

Cassie's mom felt like she was thoroughly being reprimanded for not taking better care of her daughter. She was humiliated and didn't dare tell the psychologist she was a single parent living with her boyfriend and had been the one to tell Cassie she was "a NOBODY" and not to even express things to her. She'd been the one to tell her own daughter to get out and mix with the kids on the streets. Had she really cared she would have already known the everyday pattern her own daughter now lived. It was time she was reprimanded, but instead of taking it to heart she took it out on Cassie.

When Cassie's mom came home she was really angry! She demanded of Cassie, "What are you doing? You've embarrassed me to death! I see that you are like your father, there is no hope for you. I just can't deal with you and everything else I have to deal with. The psychologist says you're skipping school, not studying like you should, and not taking your tests. Did you really think you could get by with this! Did you really think your mom wouldn't find out! I feel like tying you to a cherry tree again and making you black and blue for all to see how you're humiliating me. But since you're a big kid now, I think the best thing would be to put you in an orphanage!"

"An orphanage! How could you ever think of such a thing? Does this mean that you don't love me enough to let me stay with you?" Cassie was stunned!

"Young lady, I am very serious! You have not been going to your classes and getting your homework done and making good grades! You'll have to live in the orphanage where they can supervise you! I can't go on trying to make my living and have to police you to make sure you are going to school and doing what you should!"

You couldn't have said a worse thing to Cassie. Later Cassie would wonder was her mother just threatening her or was she really serious? But at that point Cassie thought her mother was very serious and she knew one thing for sure—she was not going to be put in an orphanage.

Many of the young people in her gang were from the orphanage and they were really aggressive. Cassie could see it was not that easy; they had their own groups and clicks in the orphanage and the strong would beat the weaker ones. This was not the place where anyone would really want to be. She couldn't even bear to think of living in a place like that.

Cassie could not help but feel a strong resentment for her mom—a resentment that her mom had been the one to throw her out into the streets to meet the ones who didn't care to study and make good grades to "bruise the good apple until a rotten spot developed." And now that the rotten spot had started to develop, her mom was just going to wash her hands of any responsibility.

She wanted to scream at her mom, "Remember, I just wanted to stay at home and study; I was content to read my books, but you were the one who threw me out on the streets. You left me to be taught by the street kids—to learn to drink and smoke, and skip classes and make bad grades—to go to discos and movies—to beg for money, or didn't you know that either? And now you want to put me in an orphanage to crumple my soul even more! But she couldn't express her feelings; she remembered that she was just a "NOBODY."

She loved her mother; she'd always loved her mom in spite of her mom's abusive treatment. She'd always hoped and dreamed that some day her mom would change—that some day she would return the love she felt for her. Her soul was bowed down with deep sorrow as the thought came to her that it wasn't just the lack of money that caused her mom to leave her at Grandpa Ivan's. Now her mom had the money that she made and the money that her grandpa sent to help out and even so—now her very own mom threatened to give her away to the orphanage. It all sunk in—hard!

The words of her mother brought her to the point of no return. She knew she was not going to go to the orphanage, so she desperately started wondering what she would do. She knew that her father didn't want her; she knew now that her mother didn't want her, and she knew that her grandmother didn't want her—only the poor, good, Grandfather Ivan, the sunshine of her life wanted her but he was just by himself, and he was so far away. She knew that her grandmother had a problem having her there—she didn't want to be a problem or a reason for their divorce, so she just decided at that point that she could see no solution in sight.

Completely heartbroken there was only one thing Cassie could think of—suicide. Then she would end all the misery in this world. She had heard that her mother had had an abortion one other time—now the thought came to her in the darkness surrounding her life that it would have been better if her mother had aborted her. Was she born only to die young?

So the decision was made. Without even saying good-bye to any of her friends, to her mother, or most of all to her dear grandpa, she decided to leave this world behind.

With downcast eyes Cassie slowly drug one foot in front of the other and ended up in a park in the middle of Sarajevo. It was a really pretty park with scattered benches among the shrubs and where usually birds fluttered and sang happily. But today it was a cold, cold park in the winter of October-November 1983. Cassie sat there on that cold, cold bench—the coldness completely enveloping her; there were no people; the trees were bare; there was no life. Her heart was so heavy it was hard to breathe; the bitter tears welled up in her eyes and spilled down her cheeks. She sobbed and sobbed in despair until no more tears could come—no one cared—no one cared; she indeed was just a "NOBODY!" Her mom had informed her with harsh words long before that she was just a "NOBODY!"

"Mom, if I'm just a 'NOBODY' then I'm just a 'Nobody's Child!'" she wanted to scream out. Today she really felt it to the depths of her soul. Someway, through it all, she'd always hoped that her mother really did love her, that one day she was going to say she was sorry for all the things she'd said and done to her—someway that hope kept her going. Now that hope was completely shattered.

At twelve years of age Cassie saw no hope surrounding her; she now sat in silence, contemplating how she would end her misery in this world. She wanted to make sure when she attempted this that it would be for sure—that she would really die; she didn't want to become an invalid; she started making a plan. There were several different ways that she could think of but she was thinking that probably the best way would be to jump in front of an electric train that served as public transportation in the city. She would throw herself in front of this train; there would be a thud; she would never know what hit her. When they found her lifeless body who would care? The misery would be gone forever. "Nobody" would be gone forever!

At the point when she was almost sure that she had it all planned, a strong idea came to her mind, "What if there really is a God!" But then she was just fighting, thinking, "It's not possible that there is a God because there is too much misery in this world and look at myself. It is just a condition without any hope. I don't believe that there is a God and if there is He probably cares only about the rich people, not about the tiny ones in trouble."

But she just couldn't get rid of the idea: "There is a God! There is a God!" She felt there was a real battle inside her—in her mind—between two voices. She thought of the three years she had spent with her mother's parents when they would bring her to church and she knew that they believed in a God but she had not personally experienced anything and honestly didn't know what to really believe.

Some in her grandparents' church, as with any other church, were all absorbed with thoughts about who was the greatest—who would get a certain position—even as the disciples in Jesus' day vied for positions next to Him. Even a young child as discerning as Cassie looked more at the reactions of people—people who could have turned her thoughts to God instead of to themselves. Their greed caused them to forget for the moment that they could indeed be the "only Bible" that some people would read. Some of these people distracted others from the real love of a real God.

Here she was living in a communist country and most of the people believed that there was no God—that it was just something for stupid people to believe in, but if you're really intelligent and educated you know that there is no God. So her grandparents were some of the very few people who believed in God. She was just so young and really didn't know what to believe.

Because of this unrest inside her —the battle going on in her, she said, "Okay, let's have a deal–if there really is a God in this world—I want You, if you really exist, to take these suicidal thoughts away and I want You to give me strength to live because I am really at the end."

She was so depressed and didn't see any light—not one single light on the horizon—it was like dark clouds around her. She didn't see any future—any hope—nothing—and she didn't know up to that point what she was really doing. She was praying and telling God, "If you really exist I want You to take these thoughts from me and give me special strength and power to live and to fight in life!"

She couldn't believe—within seconds, instantly, she felt such a power going through her body like electricity, it was something you just don't forget—ever—and she felt like she was filled with energy and ambition to live and to really accomplish something.

It was with such magnitude! She was so instantly revitalized! It had to be that God was FOR REAL! Nothing would ever tear her away from this wonderful experience that God was in control of this world! God did really care about the tiniest person. He infinitely cared about all the "Nobodies" of the world, and at this moment especially He cared about this "Nobody!" This "Nobody" suddenly became the daughter of the King—the King of the universe!

This day a whole new world of love opened for Cassie! "If God be for us, who can be against us!" What did it matter if any man or woman was Cassie's enemy—she had the greatest friend in the world—she was truly the daughter of THE KING! Her heart sang His praises.

Down through history, with the real, usually comes a counterfeit. This was no counterfeit experience. When God's name was called on in sincerity by Cassie, Satan knew once again that he was defeated. Never once would Cassie doubt the answer which came from God in such a miraculous way!

When she was praying, Cassie desperately cried for God 1) to take away her suicidal thoughts, 2) to give her the power to live, and 3) not only help her to live but to help her to become somebody special in this world not just a regular person in Yugoslavia.

Cassie just wanted to reach the top as much as possible—so then she had this special experience of God giving her a direct answer to her plea. She was thinking, "Wow! I don't know what the future will bring"—this was the first experience with God that she ever had and at that point she knew in the middle of this communist country—this unbelieving country—she knew that there is a God that cared about her! He really cared about her and it didn't matter that she was "nobody". It didn't matter that nobody wanted her. She left that cold, cold, lonesome park with the dark clouds surrounding her, her head lifted up—a spring in her step— saying, "Okay, I'm going to school and I'm going to leave this click; I'm going to study because this is the first step—to study, to get good grades, to get an education and she knew that was the real answer.

Slowly she improved in school but it was so sad that the teachers wouldn't give her high grades; for instance, if before she might have gotten a D in a subject, and now her work was as good as somebody who got an A they would not let her jump from D to A. They would give her a C like, "Oh, yes, you're *getting* better." So she was thinking, "My work is as good as this person who got an A, what more can I do?" She was also seeing that it made a big difference if your father and mother were educated. If you came from a family that was really well-off then, "Okay this is the son or daughter from doctor so and so," then they were just automatically the privileged. If you came from maybe another dedicated family "Fine, a C, or B is enough for her she's not going to come through anyway," so she was really sad about that but she couldn't change it.

This experience with God was in the late winter of 1983 and then she had several months—the spring semester of 1984 to improve her grades and finish these seven years of elementary school. Then, Grandfather Ivan, bless his heart, came to Sarajevo to talk with Cassie's mom. He said he thought that Cassie should come back to live with them. This made Cassie really happy. She loved her grandfather and now she knew that he was going to pay her way all the time. She just saw this as a little light and just hoped someway it was going to work out with her grandma. Then she found out the reason why her grandpa made this decision was because even though her mother didn't earn enough money she was still supporting all her boyfriends and going out and spending money on everything for them and needed "more money for Cassie to go to school."

Then with time they began to realize that Cassie was just the excuse to get more money and that her mom was not really spending that much money on her like she was saying. So Cassie felt strongly that it was best for her to live with her grandparents. She didn't know exactly what made them make this decision. She didn't know even if her grandmother was involved in making the decision but she did know that her Grandfather Ivan personally came from a little town in Bosnia called Doboj and he came by bus.

When Grandpa Ivan knocked on the door, Cassie saw his big smile and knew that all was going to be well again.

"Daughter, I have come to take Cassie home with us. We cannot support you any longer; we know that you have been using the hard earned money we send to you on your boyfriends instead of on Cassie. Now you are going to have to take care of things on your own. We love you and hope that things go well for you. You don't have to be concerned about Cassie's care any more; she will be safe with us!"

Cassie thought her mom was so happy to get rid of her that it was okay for her to lose money that she was trying to get from her parents because of Cassie.

Another thing that lowered Cassie's self-esteem was recalling the special friendship of a certain girlfriend. Her parents were very university-educated people; they were teachers and so on and they became good friends but when it was found out that Cassie's mother was poor, and that she was not well educated, things changed. Cassie didn't tell them— she didn't know how they found out but they told their daughter that they didn't want her to associate with Cassie any more that she was a pretty good girl but they were thinking that she was not really an appropriate friend for their daughter. Cassie was deeply troubled by this—it really lowered her self-esteem.

It was very heart-breaking for Cassie's special girlfriend to inform her that her parents wouldn't let her be friends with her anymore because her parents weren't as educated as her parents.

Cassie also was broken-hearted when she heard this. This was something that would stay in the girls' minds all their lives. Perhaps in the years to come they could someday meet each other and renew the friendships they missed as young friends.

Now, the sad experiences of living with her mother and not being able to really enjoy her home life but having to mix in the streets with the rough kids who really didn't want to study were finally over!

No longer would she have to spend time in the afternoons locked up in the school's bathroom until the bullies left the school yard!

She wouldn't have to sleep in the same room with her mother and her mother's boyfriends and have no place to really call home!

Cassie wouldn't have to beg for money on the street to support her smoking and drinking with her friends.

Besides, now that Cassie had had this "mountain top experience" with God and saw the changes she needed to make in her life, God gave her the strength to resist these bad habits so that they had no appeal to her.

So it was with great relief in June of 1984 that school was over and Cassie left Sarajevo.

In February 1984, the 14th Olympic Games were in Sarajevo. They had been building the city for several years. It gave her countrymen good working experiences to build the Olympic buildings with their skills already developed, while some of them learned trades that would benefit them in their future careers for life.

The city was really just beautiful and the people from all over the world were coming there.

Sarajevo was the center of the world for one month—it was beautifully-made, and clean! They could be so proud to be chosen for this very special event! Later Cassie's heart, as well as those of her countrymen would break to think that everything was destroyed when the ethnic wars broke out—it had been so neat and now it seemed only a dream. Cassie was so proud at that point that she was living there. She enjoyed so many things at the Olympics especially the ice skating! Had her situation in life not been so desperate at this time, this event would have been especially exhilarating.

Chapter 4
COMMON GROUND

When Cassie was in the second or third grade, eight or nine years old—many people felt that the main person actually keeping the country together was Tito. Tito was in high ranks from 1948 when Yugoslavia's independence was declared from Russian control until he died in 1981.

Originally from Croatia, Tito was born as Josip Broz. In 1920 Tito helped organize the Yugoslavian Communist Party but it was outlawed and he was sent to jail in 1928. To confuse the police after his release in 1934 he took the name Tito. He was secretary-general to the Yugoslavian Communist Party from 1937-1966 when he became the party President. During World War II he organized and led the Partisans, guerrillas who fought the German troops occupying Yugoslavia.

During World War II there were also ethnic army groups like Serbs. In Croatia, they had their own army. The Moslems had their own army and so on. They were killing each other; in addition there were Germans that were also killing. It was a big mess so what Tito was trying to do with the Communist Party, was as he said, "Look there is no God; there is no religion. You don't believe in God and if religion is not important and if we're all the same then we are all on common ground wanting to fight for a free country where we can live together. We are all equal." What he did was to organize a special group of people called Partisans; they had their own army and they were atheist. They were composed of members from many different ethnic groups.

It seemed like this was the only solution for the country and the people were very much motivated. More and more people joined the Partisans—fighting like guerillas. They were mostly in the woods and were ready to fight against the Germans, against the Italians, and against the ethnic armies like the Chetniks. The Serbs had their army group called the Chetnicks. The Croatians had their army group called the Ustochet. And then there was the Moslem army.

Tito kept tight control over the people and tolerated no opposition. In later years Cassie would be surprised to read of Tito as being a "dictator"; she just hadn't thought of him in this light, but the more she thought about it she said, "I guess he *was* a dictator since he sent people to prison who opposed him, etc."

It is interesting that in the Bible we have the Book Titus, and in Cassie's language the name Titus was Tito. In 1963 Tito made himself president for life and later encouraged some economic and political freedom. It was during this economic and political freedom period that Cassie would remember Tito. Naturally she remembered him mostly because of what the adults said about him. According to their way of thinking Tito had an extremely strong personality and was keeping Yugoslavia together.

While he was President for 35 years Tito tried to establish very good relationships with different world countries. He was generally well-received all over the world, visiting many different Presidents, and the Presidents from other countries really seemed to like him. It seemed he had a very good diplomatic way of dealing with many heads of state. The country was poor and totally destroyed from World War II, so his strategy was to borrow money from all these countries to build up the country. During these many years of communism that Cassie remembered, financially-wise, Yugoslavia seemed not really that bad at all.

Cassie remembered her grandparents telling that the dino which was the monetary unit in Yugoslavia in the 1960's and 1970's was stronger than the schilling in Austria which was considered almost like the best European country and Yugoslavia was really prospering.

The social system seemed very good to many people in Yugoslavia; if you were unemployed you would get unemployment money—it was typical for communist countries according to some, that you could never really get rich. You could work like a slave but you could never get rich. But neither would you be so poor that you had to live as a homeless person on the streets.

As Tito grew older and older and reached the age of eighty he became very sick and went to the hospital. The whole country suddenly came under what they felt was a cloud of depression.

Cassie remembers the people were so scared, so worried. Most people were saying, "If Tito dies we are going to be in great trouble." Cassie didn't understand why they thought they would be in trouble but she could sense something was going to happen. He died very soon and many of the people felt this was actually when all the troubles started.

Now that Tito was dead the countries that had let him borrow the money for his country now felt there was no diplomatic, stable person in the presidency and suddenly the finances and the economy started to quickly go down and down.

The death of Tito to the people of those times in that country was like the sudden death of President Kennedy in the United States when many people felt like a great cloud of depression was over them and there was a terrifying sense of not knowing what was ahead—the fear of the unknown came over them.

For the little girl that Cassie was, feeling secure with the general feelings of her countrymen and the death of this stabilizing man for her country brought great fear. Cassie would remember times when they would go to the supermarket to try to buy groceries, they would go in the morning to buy bread for a certain price and then many times when they would go in the afternoon it would already be more expensive—inflation was very, very high and growing so very fast. You almost couldn't keep up with the inflation.

The year that Tito died was the year when Cassie left to live with her mother in Sarajevo and this was the time when the economy really started to go more and more down and slowly many different parties started to develop—all these ethnic issues that were actually more or less in the roots started slowly to come up and up and up. It seems when there is a financial problem then suddenly many different problems arise.

But there was another thing happening when Cassie was in first grade and six years old, when the country was still deep in communism. It was the custom that the students would be taken into the Pioneers—the first step of getting into the Communist Party.

One day the teacher said to the Pioneers, "Children, guess what! Today you are going to be given a special gift! Just look at this special Partisan hat. Oh, look at the pretty red star on it." And the kids would ooh and aah over their pretty hats—the red star had 5 points, typical of the Yugoslavia Partisan symbol.

"Oh, and guess what else—tomorrow we are all going to get to go on a special trip!" The kids clapped their hands with glee—it would be great fun to go on a field trip they thought.

Then an organized excursion would be made for kids to visit concentration camps.

Cassie was told that in World War II there were many organizations killing people of different ethnic backgrounds. Mainly Germany killed thousands of people in gas chambers. After War War II concentration camps were erected as memory places for school-organized excursions. It seemed to Cassie that it now came to a point of brain-washing that they would bring the kids to camps and show how the Germans killed in a very terrible way. They developed in kids a negative attitude toward Germany. They tried to put in very young minds that communism was the way to go—that communism was the only way of living where you really could live freely and could develop freely.

Cassie would later say, "I tell you it's so sad but it's really true when you're born in that society when you hear this and they don't come as monsters to you, they believe somehow in this themselves and then brain-washing happens at a very early age to the people as kids." Somehow the kids would develop very negative attitudes about the Western countries and she thought this was what they basically wanted to emphasize. It was really so terrible for her to watch films that they had showing these terrible skeletons of people and the way people were molested and killed. The kids had these thoughts in their heads—these terrible scenes and she wondered, "Is this a healthy way to teach these kids at seven or eight years old?" Anyway this was part of the program.

The other thing she especially remembered was when you were about fourteen or fifteen years of age there was a class in the first year of high school—a class to show the many different kinds of weapons and how to put them together and take them apart—different types of military equipment and how they worked. At that point it was very normal to her, she didn't know anything different, to learn how the tanks work—the theory and also the practical part to go to a special place to learn to shoot guns. If you would refuse this on a religious basis they would not respect that. If you didn't finish the class you couldn't finish high school. It meant your education at fourteen years of age would end if you didn't want to do anything with weapons.

Every single child had to go through formal education because they wanted to brain-wash them in communist ways about evolution and that there was no God, so if you would not be there in school you would not be exposed to that and they wouldn't want that.

When they were in the first year of high school they had communist science and that subject was really something. They had to study all the communist beginnings of such communist leaders as Marx, Lenin and Stalin—their biographies and books that they wrote—their philosophies and other people's philosophies—it was heavy. They were really working hard on it. Already in the beginning of high school you could be a member of the communist party and only if you were a member of the party could you be considered to be the president of the youth organization or some position. To be able to have many different kinds of positions at the university you were required to be a member of the communist party.

To be a person who believed in God and who wanted to be faithful was really a trial in a communist country. Later when she would think of all the kindergarten schools, high schools, colleges, and universities almost on every corner from many different denominations in countries that had freedom of religion she was amazed, "Those kids don't even know everything is so perfect. You can keep your religion. You don't have to worry about anything, it's such a normal everyday thing for them!" But for her to see these many schools to choose from, it was always something very special. What a special blessing!

Chapter 5

GRANDPA'S SURPRISE
FROM THE STREETS TO SAFETY

In 1984 dear Grandpa Ivan came to tell his daughter that they could no longer send her money "to take care of Cassie" when they had found out that she was really using this money on her boyfriends. And he told her that he had come to take Cassie home to live with them.

Cassie's mom didn't hesitate. She'd already been shamed by the school psychologist for not taking better care of Cassie. She realized that her dad now knew that the "money for Cassie" had only been an excuse to get money.

Cassie's mom was rather speechless—she knew her dad read right through her. And it really would be a relief to let Cassie go live with her dad and mom—then she could be free to live without the added responsibility.

It didn't take Cassie long to pack up her few belongings. Talk about relief! It was absolutely marvelous for Cassie to think about getting away from the streets and to think about living with Grandpa Ivan.

Her heart sang to be with Grandpa Ivan again, riding along beside him, leaving the city where so much trouble was in the air. As they rode along Grandpa began to lay out a plan for Cassie to be able to continue her school.

It was decided that Cassie was going to go back to her grandparents. They didn't live any more in the little town called Doboj. At that point they retired and wanted to go back to live where they were from, a little village in Bosnia about twenty miles away from Banja Luka.

During the short time that Cassie had lived with her mom she'd gone through some of the roughest times a child could go through. And with the deal of giving her away to the orphanage still fresh in her mind she'd now come to fully realize her mom's true feelings.

Yes, it's true, only the caged know what true freedom really is. Like a butterfly, flying in the fresh blue sky, sipping nectar from one beautiful, fragrant flower to another—she was free once more. "Oh, Grandpa, you came just in time, "Did you know Mom was going to put me in the orphanage?" The bitter tears came with a sudden rush!

"No, Dear Child, no! My Cassie would never be put in an orphanage. I would never let this happen! It's okay now. You never have to think of that again—never!" Grandpa stroked her soft brown hair and wiped a big tear away with his thumb. "But what about Grandma. She won't like for me to stay there with you, will she! I don't want to cause any trouble."

"Oh, I've been thinking, and I've been praying and I think I have a good plan. As far as your grandma's feelings, you are grown up now, she doesn't have to worry about baby-sitting a young child. Now you can help to take care of her. I've already discussed my plan with her and she agrees. Besides, she was going through a lot of changes in her life when you were there last. Times have changed. She knows you're a 'good apple'." And they both flashed a knowing look at each other and burst out with a big laugh. Cassie had a cute way of wrinkling up her nose and giving a slight wink of her eye when she laughed.

"This is my plan, see what you think; your grandma likes the idea too. Since we live in this little village about twenty miles from school and have no daily transportation, we thought we'd rent you a room. Fortunately we found a room to rent from an elderly sister from the church. This lady's little home is very close to the regular school and happily the music school is very close by, also. You can go to school each day and then come home on the weekends to be with us!"

This was a new idea completely for Cassie. She'd never even thought of living by herself but she knew Grandpa would only make the best of plans.

"You just wait and see. I think you'll like it really well. But first, let's just get home and then we can take you to your room."

Everything was new for Cassie. She felt good that her grandparents didn't have to work so hard in their sweater factory. She felt good that they were able to go back to live where they were from and it sounded like a neat plan to have her own room at school.

Little grandma came out of the house smiling, with open arms, when they reached "home." Just seeing her looking older sent a surge of love over Cassie. They both hugged each other close. Grandma kept saying, "Just look at you—you're so much taller than when we saw you last. You've grown so big!"

"Well, come on in, Cassie, Grandma has bought some special treats for you."

Grandma already had the table set with a real feast of some of Cassie's favorites. They topped it all off with a special dessert made from sweet dough wrapped around sweet plums. These plums were in much demand in Europe.

Cassie was a polite little lady and thanked her grandma profusely for a wonderful meal before she helped her do the dishes.

They talked about the elderly sister whose home they would soon bring Cassie to in order for her to be able to go to school. They talked way up into the night about many things from school to the release from street life. And finally eyes grew too weary to stay up any longer. It had been a long day of travel to new surroundings.

Cassie slipped into her pretty, white embroidered gown that Grandma had bought. Grandma even had some new, pink, washcloth mittens for Cassie to take with her to her school home. Washcloth "mittens" was a tradition in their country.

"Good-night—sweet dreams," Cassie's voice chimed to Grandma and Grandpa and they couldn't help but feel the difference they had made.

"Good-night, Princess," Grandpa bid her.

"Good-night grown-up Cassie," Grandma smiled.

It was a wonderful feeling to slip between the fresh-smelling clean sheets that had been hung in the fresh air and sunshine today, and the comforter above her. Cassie's weary mind felt real peace. She caught a sliver of moonlight from a window overhead and thinking about this same moonlight with a whole different picture for the street kids she poured out a prayer of thanks from her heart to the REAL God who had helped her through so much! She knew it would be a whole new life—a whole new life climbing Jacob's ladder from trouble to peace because she'd learned there was a ladder reaching from Earth to Heaven with angels going up and down bringing special strength for each new day!

It didn't take long for the sun to come up and along with it the tantalizing smell of Grandma's breakfast.

"Well, how about if we go take a look at your new home, Cassie?" Grandpa picked up her belongings and the new things Grandma had put together for her.

The twenty miles went rather slowly as the bus made it's stops. And then they had a little walk to the place where Cassie was to stay.

It was a pretty, little, white cottage where Sister Lily lived and a few of summer's bright, fragrant flowers still lingered. Setting his heavy suitcase down Grandpa knocked on the door. Sister Lily was waiting; she smiled broadly and made Cassie feel very welcome.

Sister Lily motioned for them to sit down, brought a little glass of juice for each of them and a piece of cake. Then she took them to Cassie's bed and showed them the closet where she could put her belongings.

After a short stay the grandparents took Cassie by the school. Grandpa had already gotten Cassie's acceptance at the music school as well as the elementary school. Tomorrow Cassie would start 8th grade. As she met new friends she discovered quite a difference between them and her street friends. She felt safe here and each day gave God thanks for working out plans as He had. She enjoyed school and looked forward to going to her little "home" where she could study and read more. Grandma's pretty white sheets and soft down-filled comforter made her bed feel like home.

But it was extra special to go "home" for the weekends—to laugh and talk with Grandpa Ivan and Grandma, too.

The first day Cassie met her violin instructor at the music school he left her alone for a few minutes with her violin as he took care of some other details.

A smile played around Cassie's lips as she ran her hand lightly over the beautiful, satiny-smooth finish on the wood of the violin. It's curves were so gentle. She took the bow and lightly ran it across the violin strings then looked up to see the instructor looking at her, "You're a natural," he said. Cassie wanted to be "a natural"—she really enjoyed her violin lessons. If only her instructor could know the songs she could play about the dark valleys as well as the bright splashes of sunlight on her pathway—what a song she could play!

So it was that at the age of only 13 Cassie was really on her own here in the eighth grade. And happily she now was able to take violin classes! She would live there during the week and then on weekends she would take the bus to go back to the village where her grandparents lived, spend the weekend there and then usually by Sunday evening or Monday morning take the bus again to travel back to Banja Luka. During the week she would just eat sandwiches or maybe baked potatoes—not very nutritional meals. It would really be special to have some REAL food on the weekends at her grandparents home.

She lived at this rented room until she finished the eighth grade which ended elementary school in Yugoslavia.

It didn't seem long at all until it was 8th grade graduation day! Of course it was a communist regime and her class motto and class goal would have read much differently had she graduated from a Christian school, but in her heart she felt God's blessing for each hour of life itself. No one really knew how close she'd been to death!

Chapter 6

A STRANGE DREAM THAT CHANGED EVERYTHING!

There was a few weeks break from school after her eighth grade graduation. It was good to be at home with Grandma and Grandpa once again. Besides that, she had time to be with her friends again—her friends were her books!

But the weeks went by quickly and before she knew it, it was time to enroll in high school. Once again she would be at the bottom working up—a freshman. She met other friends besides her books at the high school and increasingly became a better and better student—one of the best students in her grades; her goal was to be the best; she saw that she really could achieve and it was a good feeling.

Cassie would go to church with her grandparents in Banja Luka. This was the only church around. The people would travel many, many miles to get to church. She went with her grandparents to church but she didn't fully understand what they were really telling her about God. She believed—how could she not believe after her awesome experience the day she asked God to prove that there was a REAL God— but she needed to really get to know Him. She needed a special experience with God and what she saw in the church was that it was just dead. They would fight among each other about the positions, about who was going to be the elder, who was going to have a higher position, etc.

The youth were definitely not living like the church doctrines taught. They would smoke, and drink and go places that people of her church wouldn't go and they were not really interested in church. As long as they were with their parents they felt like they had to go to church but when they went on their own they would just leave. And so most of the people were old people and she had somehow the impression that being a believer was more for the old people especially if you were a young person in a communist country where you wanted to get an education and to accomplish something. If you were a believer you were not going to get that far. If you were lucky you might get some trade and try to earn something that way but to get a high education if you were a faithful believer it would really be almost a miracle.

Unfortunately she would hear from some sisters in the church recommending that she wait until she was finished with schooling and then make a decision for Jesus. She was thinking that year, "I know that God exists and I believe in a God and probably that's enough and then when I get really retired I will become a believer." So she would go to church but she didn't really enjoy it because "it was so dead." But she had to go because of her grandparents.

She became more and more involved with school until, eventually, she was one of the best students and was recommended to be the president of the youth of the whole school. The only problem was she was not in the communist party. At that point she was thinking, "Yeah, who really cares; I'm not actually baptized in the church and I don't really believe in these communist beliefs but if its going to help me to accomplish something in my career I'm going to do it." So she became a member of the communist party but interestingly enough the thing was that they misspelled her name, so officially, because of that mistake she was never actually a member. For some reason she was someway happy and never asked them to correct her name. She was thinking maybe that's like a providence.

Cassie lay awake at night, so excited by the thought that her name was being suggested to be the youth leader of her school that she could hardly sleep. She had all kinds of ideas she wished to promote if she won this position.

The morning that the announcement was to be made as to who won the position Cassie was up early singing with the birds. When it was announced that Cassie was the new youth leader, she could hardly believe her ears.

The way home seemed so very long. Finally, she burst in the door, "Guess what! I am the youth leader of the school!"

Grandma and Grandpa clapped their hands. A big smile broke over Grandpa's face and tears of happiness filled their eyes. Their very own granddaughter was leader of the youth group! What a special feeling! Grandpa's prayers would be for special wisdom for Cassie in her new and important role.

Suddenly Cassie became the president of the youth group—suddenly she was in the high society among the youth. She would be there in the meetings with the youth leaders from the school, and the whole city of Banja Luka and they would meet and discuss things. She felt really good about herself and was planning on entering the university and finishing her education there.

She was so eager to get her education that she decided to do two years in one year, so she finished the third year and the fourth year of high school in one year and she graduated when she was 17.

Time seemed to fly by so quickly. After finishing high school she had great plans. First she had to take a test and if she passed the test they were going to take her into the university. It was a happy day when she came home and was able to tell her grandparents, "Guess what! I passed the big test, now I can register at the university."

Grandma and Grandpa were very happy for her! Especially Grandpa was so proud that Cassie was doing so well in school. She was not only a "good apple"—she was the "apple of his eye." He was so thankful that he had persevered and rescued her from the streets where her mother had sent her. He would never regret putting forth the extra effort to bring her back into his household to see that she was able to finish elementary school, and then high school. She stood very tall in his eyes. More than anyone else he had listened to Cassie's heart's desires, her times in the valleys and her times on the mountain tops. He thanked God for making the plans for her life.

So it was that in June of 1988, Cassie put on her favorite dress and freshly polished shoes and mingled with the crowd of students applying for school at the university.

The school would start with lectures in October 1988; this was very typical in Yugoslavia that if you were a freshman you would start in October and if you were in the second, third, or fourth year you would start in September

"Look at you! You're only 17. You're still just a young teenager, and soon you will be a student at the university," laughed Grandpa.

Cassie was very, very, very proud of herself. At 17 she had accomplished what she thought she wanted to accomplish and in a few months she was going to be a freshman. She was "really full of herself." Now she had a few months of vacation ahead of her before she would start the school year at the university and she was deciding what she would do during that vacation.

In Yugoslavia you didn't have a great chance to work as a young person; the unemployment rate was so high—there were barely enough working places for the people so they didn't have much to offer students during vacation. Some young people who would have connections would try to find work at the Adriatic coast during the summer season, there were so many tourists coming from different countries.

In earlier years Cassie's grandmother would often take her to the Adriatic Coast which was usually mild, with a sunny climate much like Italy. The coast was long and pleasant—a popular resort area that was fairly inexpensive for the people who lived there. Rising from the coastal strip were rugged mountains that had such a harsh climate where few people lived. Croatia was a crescent-shaped area extending along the Sava River, and the coast. Bosnia was in the center of this crescent.

For a European spending a vacation, the Adriatic coast offered probably one of the cheapest ways of spending a vacation but you would really have to know someone to help you get there because everything goes through the connection. When she heard of how it was in the States her heart could almost not believe the opportunities—if you want to work you could usually find work, maybe not what you really wanted but you could work and earn money. When she heard that it didn't matter what your age was if you were a high school student you could usually find a few hours here, a few hours there, it seemed such a privilege. "Do the teenagers really know what a blessing it is to have this opportunity to work?" she wondered, because she wanted to work but she didn't have any chance to do so.

Her grandparents' church was organizing a meeting for the youth in August of 1988 in Croatia. The church had bought a little house in a beautiful, quiet place in the mountains. They would organize programs for young people who would come from all different parts of Yugoslavia and stay for two weeks and get to know each other. Cassie decided she would go there, little knowing that this was a very essential turning point in her life.

The Lord provided that there were many other young people there and most of them who came to this particular meeting were freshly baptized, converted young people and they were just glowing—she could really see that the love of God meant so much to them—they were so special; they were so pure and dedicated and she was so impressed.

They would sit on a hillside overlooking valleys and look up at the grandeur of the mountains. It was so peaceful. Often they would sing special songs of Jesus love—songs that they would never forget. They could almost see Jesus tenderly caring for His flock of sheep on the green hillsides and leading them beside the still waters. They could see themselves as the lost sheep—maybe not even realizing that they were lost—just nibbling here and there without sensing that they were getting farther and farther away from the Shepherd and His safety. Suddenly when danger came they realized they were all alone. What a wonder it was when all the rest of the flock were now back home and safe from the storms and dangers of the night, in their folds, that the Shepherd knew exactly which ones were missing. As He would go out in the darkness of the night, His sandaled feet would be cut with sharp rocks and His flesh would be torn with briars but He never gave up until He brought the very last lost sheep safely home.

There would be songs of the "Rock of Ages," of what a "Mighty Fortress Is Our God."

Looking up at the rocky mountains reaching up to the blue skies and on up to Heaven brought a feeling of God's awesome power—His stability and His protection.

Cassie marveled as she heard about the Son of God leaving the splendor of Heaven to come to a dark world to save His brothers and sisters. For Him there was no escape—His blood would be spilled, the wages of sin, as a ransom for any who would accept the debt He paid. All His life on Earth He was headed for a cruel, early death.

Sitting in the quiet countryside, Cassie absorbed all she was learning about a Man who had come to save her. It wasn't that He could not, it was that He would not escape shedding His blood to save His people. Her heart went out in total commitment to accept His sacrifice for her. A certain peace came over her that she would carry throughout her life. From now on when any sadness or quandary as to what to do would come she would repeat, "Jesus knows all about it." "All things beautiful will come in His time."

Little did Cassie know that soon, for her, this choice of commitment to Him, no matter what, would mean the difference of her life or death.

She had never seen or heard young people with such faith and purpose in their lives. She had seen maybe an old person but never a young person her age who was so excited about God; she was totally like in a dream during those two weeks. One thing she knew for sure was that she wanted to have this experience, too. It was just so special that she wanted to have it.

These young people may never have completely realized what a positive influence they were to each other and especially to those who were not yet baptized. But in Heaven they will see for themselves those they met during those two weeks and hear what an influence they were on other's lives.

There will be many stars glittering on their crowns that they never even thought about at that time—a star for Cassie—and the stars on Cassie's crown down through her future as she influenced others.

After two weeks Cassie went home and excitedly told her grandparents of all her wonderful experiences at this camp.

"Grandma and Grandpa, I want to be baptized!" Her face was glowing as she spoke these words.

Grandpa and Grandma could see a real difference in this experience of hers and they were so very happy for Cassie.

On a beautiful day—September 10, 1988, Cassie's sparkling eyes reflected the love she felt from above—as the minister baptized her, a symbol of dying from sins and being raised to a new life. As she wiped the water from her eyes her face was aglow. She'd made this important step not because she'd been made to but because she really wanted to. It was just the beginning of a new way of life but it was a wonderful, wonderful day to remember!

Once again, in October, she was among the crowds of students, this time at the university. It felt so good to be a freshman in the university. For the next few weeks she studied hard and was making such good grades. With her bright smile and winning ways she was making new friends. Her bright, thoughtful mind was like a sponge absorbing and holding onto all the new things she was learning each day!

This was October 1988 but at the end of October after she'd only gone to school for about a month and was doing so well in her studies, one night she fell asleep, the same as any other night. She never suspected that this night would be any different.

As she was sleeping, suddenly she had a dream— she had a dream that changed everything. In her dream she saw a dragon on the left-hand side coming toward her and spitting fire, having the intention to really swallow her up—to kill her. On the right-hand side she saw a beautiful shinning angel in white standing and telling her with words she could not forget, "Cassie, you should leave this university. This is going to bring you into disaster." This was the end of the dream. She awoke and knew there was something really significant about this dream. It was not a regular dream; it was something she just knew was from God—God letting her know that something was going to happen, that she needed to get out. But she was thinking, "Lord, I am finally on the top; I'm going to pursue this career. You have saved me from this misery and now I am at the university and I want to study and become *somebody* and You are telling me that I should leave it—to do what?" She didn't know what, but she knew just a few weeks ago she made a commitment that she would follow the Lord and that meant that she would trust Him and follow Him even though she didn't understand—she would go in faith. Path unseen—future unknown—like Abraham of old she would go where He would lead. Sheep of His pasture she knew His voice.

Cassie was stoic but felt, "How am I going to tell my family. They're going to think I'm kind of crazy. I've been doing so much to get to the university and finally made it and then suddenly I'm leaving! Oh, no!" But she had made a resolution and gave thanks to God for a warning that she couldn't begin to understand now, but she made a firm determination to follow His plans. Her choice to follow His plans would be very significant and she would plainly see the reason for the warning in the days to come. A storm was brewing that would be a shock to many.

But it didn't matter how she felt, she knew she had to do it; it was right and she had to tell the others she was leaving and the reason why. They may have felt she was just crazy—they weren't really saying anything to change her mind because they knew when she said something she usually did it, or maybe it was because they were also thinking it was God's will. It would not be long until they would see for themselves why this dream came to Cassie. God had a special plan for her life—her whole future was hanging on what she would do next! Life or death was hanging in the balance for Cassie—her reaction to the warning in the dream—her choice would make the difference.

Chapter 7

FALLING IN LOVE—
BLUE EYES AND BLONDE HAIR

Cassie did not hesitate. She must leave the university. It wasn't easy explaining why she was leaving.

"Because of a dream? Are you crazy—we all have dreams. It was just a dream that's all—forget all about it! Are you superstitious!" Some would not understand.

Of course it was a shock for Grandma and Grandpa to see Cassie coming home—just when she was starting to do so well at the university. But with Cassie's determination they knew it must have really been some special dream. And if she had the faith to know that God was taking care of it all they must have that faith too.

When Cassie left the university she went to live in this tiny village in the house of her grandparents. What do you do when you're 17 and in that predicament? Hadn't one of her prayers at the time when she planned her suicide been to not just be a regular person in Yugoslavia but to really be someone special to be used of God. She felt like her dreams were falling apart; she was in that tiny village without anything—no library, no nothing to continue her education. It was not like the USA—it was Eastern Europe, you didn't have a car, you didn't have work, you didn't have anything.

Sure enough she was studying and studying and reading; time went on and on, January came and February, March, and nothing was happening.

Some people started to try to match her with someone so she could get married but there was no one with whom she was really interested. They said, "Yeah, Cassie, you're 18 and you're not studying, it's time for you to get married; you have a high school education."

But she was thinking, "My! I don't really feel like I've accomplished anything that I wanted and anyway there is no man around in whom I am really interested."

She felt impressed that she just wanted to leave to go some other place but she didn't know where to go. She was limited by finances, a place to stay in another country, a language she could learn, etc.

"Cassie, do you remember Sophia the student who used to work with us in our sweater business? She was a good worker and then she got married. They went to Australia and she writes that she's really enjoying it there."

This sparked an interest in Cassie and she said, "Yes, Australia! I would like to go there. I've heard many interesting things about Australia!"

So she wrote a letter to this friend asking if she would be willing to write an invitation letter because that was the only way for her to get into that country.

As the days went by Cassie got an answer from the friend saying she would be happy to send an invitation. This was already like June or July 1989 and she was thinking that was the way to go. "I'm leaving for Australia!"

After thinking about it more her grandparents were not so happy. They said, "Oh, you cannot do that, you know we're so old and that's so far and we're never going to see each other anymore."

Cassie pondered, "Yeah, but I just have to look at my future, too."

In the end of August 1989 suddenly Grandfather said, "What do you think about going to Austria to the school there to study German?"

"Yeah, I can do that too, it sounds interesting." Cassie was now thinking of her alternatives. Her mother who was living in Sarajevo had come to the point she couldn't really support herself anymore and decided to emigrate to Germany, so she was living there; she met a man and they got married. She told Cassie's grandfather about the school and said that she would be willing to pay the tuition for her.

That was a surprise to Cassie and she responded, "Okay, it sounds good to me."

Very soon, in about ten days or so, Cassie packed her belongings and said good-bye to Grandma and Grandpa once more as the train pulled out from their little village. She was already on the train travelling from Banja Luka to Salzburg in Austria. This was the first week of September 1989 and then she had to go a little further to a little village where the school was, about forty miles from Salzburg.

Cassie was so impressed with Austria. It was so beautiful and clean. For some reason that she couldn't understand, in Eastern European countries it seemed it was very typical that dirt was everywhere, the people were just used to throwing garbage through the window when they were travelling—everything was so dirty. In Austria it seemed like Eden, it was so nice and clean and taken care of so well.

When she started to school there she didn't know one single word of German. She had learned a little bit of English in the school she attended before this. She was trying to teach herself English but she realized soon that her English was so poor. She could say the basics—what her name was, "Good morning" and "Good Evening," when she was born, where she was born, and how old she was, but not really much more.

It was interesting that in that school most of the students came from the States and the remaining were from all over Eastern Europe, Iceland, England, Spain, France—from everywhere. She had a rather funny experience in the first or second week. She could understand that all the students had to go some place and she understood the time that they were to meet, but she didn't understand where they were going to go so she dressed in a casual dress and walking shoes, and took her purse. Then they boarded the bus and departed. After travelling awhile they ended up in the middle of the beautiful Alpine mountains and then she realized that actually the plan was to go for a hiking day. She realized she was totally inappropriately dressed for that project but she was glad that at least she didn't wear high heels or it would have been even worse.

When she had this experience she got so mad at herself that she said, "No, I'm going to study like crazy to learn this language; I don't want to ever have this happen to me again. I don't know what someone's telling me. I tell you I was so determined that I studied hard; I was picking up this language and within two months I was really able to understand the church service and everything, and even when I would go into some missionary work with the people and the students, and go door to door I could understand the people; it was just so fast that after one year I was really able to write letters, and to communicate well."

But then there were some additional things that would be good to study and since her mother was willing to pay also for the second year she decided to stay there to study German.

During the first year there she met a young man (he was actually ten years older than she was) who was studying theology. Heinrich was German and she thought he was cute; he had blue eyes and blonde hair, and a beard. She always liked men with blue eyes and blonde hair so she was thinking, "Wow, this is great!"

Sometimes Cassie and Heinrich would take long walks together. When they'd see each other in the hallways at school they'd break into big smiles and merrily chat together. As the days and nights went by they could hardly wait to see each other again. They'd wake up at nights their hearts beating fast and they could hardly wait for daybreak to get the chance to see each other again. Before they knew it they'd really fallen in love with each other!

One day when they went for a walk there seemed to be something really special in the air. They were laughing and talking together when he took her hands and turned her to face him, "Oh, Cassie, the days grow so long without you. You are so much fun to be with and I love you so very much. I just can't see myself without you. Will you marry me?"

He looked deep into her brown eyes. Every second seemed like an eternity until as if in a dream he heard her say, "Me, too, I love you! I don't want to be without you, either."

He drew her closer and their lips barely touched. Then their arms went around each other tightly and they sealed their love with a real kiss. Realizing the intensity of the moment, she blushed as she looked around to see if anyone was noticing. They were still all alone.

"We'd better go back to the school, it's getting late," she stammered nervously, her heart fluttering.

Each time they had a chance to see each other they started making wedding plans.

Cassie was only nineteen at that point. They went to visit his parents and he also met her mother in Germany where her mother and her husband met his parents, too. The two sets of parents were not living that far from each other. It was fun going on that special bus trip. They were both nervous as they tried to put on their best manners to impress the parents. The parents remembered such a time in their younger days and looked at each other knowingly. They thought the two were a great-looking couple.

As they went back to school and the regular routine, suddenly reality set in. Cassie realized the seriousness of marriage and she knew they had many problems that they had started to fight about. At first they were very happy but more and more they were not happy. In May 1989 before she finished her first year, they were engaged to get married in August, thinking that they could reconcile their differences.

Since both of them were students they needed money so during the vacation he would work in Germany. Of course they were in Western Europe now and a person could find work; this was not a problem any more.

Then there were some students from Switzerland who were studying in the school and Cassie became acquainted with them and asked about the possibility of working in Switzerland because in Switzerland you would get the best wages. These friends found a job for her in Switzerland. She was thinking, "He's going to work in Germany. I'm going to work in Switzerland; we will earn a good nestegg then in August we will be getting married."

The only way for them to correspond was to talk on the phone and they finished wedding plans by phone. Her friends who had helped her get this job in Switzerland (he was in theology and she was in physical therapy) were such a big help. The lady offered to lend Cassie her wedding dress—it was so pretty; Cassie would try it on several times and look at herself in the mirror, dreaming of her wedding day. Finally, everything was more or less planned for the wedding. It was fun deciding on the flowers and the colors her bridesmaids would be wearing, etc., etc.—weddings could be quite elaborate in their country.

During this time that she was working in Switzerland it was a neat experience. Swiss people not only helped her to find a job but then found a church family with three kids—the interesting thing was that the bride was Yugoslavian, too, and he was Swiss.

They were willing to take her into their home for one month and let her stay with them while she was working. She was working at a hospital; their house was in walking distance from the hospital and it was a nice neighborhood. This was really very neat, they were so nice and friendly, and she was just thrilled that she could spend this time of work in such a nice environment.

But while she was there for this one month there were things happening—her fiance really didn't find a job; it seemed he really was not that interested in finding a job and she was thinking, "I don't know; I'm really working hard and he seems to be kind of lazy." She grew a little bit concerned that she was going to be the one to support the whole family in the end.

Then something else happened that made a big impression on her mind. In Austria there was a pastor's family—the pastor was killed in an accident leaving his wife and two children behind. His wife didn't have any education so now she had small children to support and not really any profession to get any job. She just worked at whatever small jobs she could find.

Now Cassie was thinking, "Yeah, everything is so nice and cute when you get married but what if something happens and you don't have any profession?"

She didn't want to be a cleaning lady or something like that. She wanted to be a professional. This accident caused her to realize that somehow she was more and more not really sure that she wanted to really get married, yet. One of the final points was that her boyfriend was really suffering from ups and downs. She would say he was probably bipolar, this was what was very common there. One day he would really be up on the mountain and wanted to do this and that—but the next day he was down, depressed. She was thinking she really didn't think she wanted to be married to this type of person. Trying to understand this type of person made her so sick that she realized she didn't want to get married. She also thought about some other things; they had some other difficulties where she was thinking he really wanted to be too domineering. Finally she got up her nerve to call him and say she thought it was really better that they didn't get married then. Of course this was a heartache for him but he couldn't help but see the differences also and inside really knew they should spend more time in getting to know each other.

They postponed their wedding but they were somehow still together. Then she came back from Switzerland and still continued to work at the school in Austria to earn some money. And then she entered into the second year of study of the German language. Her boyfriend was also there. They were kind of like together but she could see more and more that they were not really for each other. She was just seeing so many things—she wanted to have a profession and then the infatuation was gone and she could really see the reality that she couldn't deal with, this bipolar personality that it was too difficult and it made her so sick.

Once she got so sick that she was thinking she was having a heart attack and went to a doctor who helped her to realize she didn't have a heart attack but the symptoms were almost the same. She had such tension in her neck that it went into her heart. Later, when she was in nursing school, she learned that if you're under that kind of stress it can stimulate your heart to act like you're getting an attack but everything is okay at that moment with your heart.

Then she told her grandparents that she didn't think she wanted to marry her fiance and they said, "Oh, no, you cannot do that, you have been together for so long; if you leave him no one is going to marry you." Cassie felt that this again was the mentality there in Yugoslavia that if you would have a boyfriend and leave him it would not be very easy to get another boyfriend. But she told them it was not like they were sleeping together or anything like that but for some reason they were thinking she should get married. But she said, "No, I'm not going to do that!"

Cassie's mother said the same thing as her grandparents did. Finally she made the decision that they should break up totally and at that moment she applied for nursing school in Austria and also in Germany to see what each offered.

Her mother was very upset because she liked the boyfriend and thought he was a nice guy and that he did the best that he could and she said, "Oh, no, you cannot do this; he is such a good guy and he's going to be a pastor and you can live here in Germany and have a good life—what are you going to do? Who's going to take care of you? I don't want to take care of you. I paid those two years and that's it. If you really leave him and then you get in to trouble that you need money or space to live don't come to me, I don't want to hear about you any more."

Once more it seemed to Cassie that her mother was more worried about money than she was about Cassie herself and the choices she wanted. Cassie said, "Okay." She then determined in her mind that even if she would die on the street that she would not ask her mother for one penny. She knew that it was not God's will for them to get married and this would be a very, very unhappy marriage.

She broke up in May 1991, and then in June she graduated from this school in Austria and applied for nursing school. Now she got an answer from both schools in Austria and in Germany that they wanted to take her but the problem was Germany didn't want to give her a visa to study in Germany but the Austrians did give her one, so she decided to continue her studies in Austria; it was in Salzburg and she was very excited.

Chapter 8

THE MEANING OF THE DREAM BECOMES AMAZINGLY CLEAR

Cassie applied again to go to Switzerland to work over the summer and she spent two months working there and spending the time also with the family she was with the year before.

September came and it was time to go back again to Austria to the nursing school. She was really grateful and excited. The Catholic church was very, very dominant in Austria and the nursing school in Salzburg was one of the formal Catholic schools. At that time it was not a part of the government schools but the Catholic system still had a great deal of influence there. There were two dorms for the nurses, one was led by secular leadership and the other by Catholic nurses.

Since Cassie was a protestant she was thinking, "Wow, I want to go to the Red Cross one that is secular," but they were full and couldn't take her so she had to go to the Catholic one. Afterwards she realized that it didn't really matter—it was not like a test that they were influenced by whether you went to mass or whatever. They did have their Catholic rituals and different masses and procedures and you could have attended them if you wished but you were not forced to do it. She was really grateful for that, now she was eagerly studying a lot and was getting good grades. She almost couldn't believe she was doing so well because she was so worried about studying in a foreign language. Even though she felt very comfortable with the German language she never went to a school that spoke German and she knew that they often liked to speak in dialects. Because she was worried they might start speaking in dialects that she wouldn't be able to understand she bought a cassette recorder.

The first week she started to tape the lectures because she was thinking she wouldn't be able to understand, but then after a few days she realized it was really not a problem at all and she stopped recording. She was really grateful that God opened this opportunity to her to be able to study this language this well and also to study nursing. She really wanted to become a nurse and she thought it was like God really gave her this desire of her heart.

It was a very, very busy time, not only classes in school but also a great deal of practice in the hospital then again studying, and tests. It was very intense, they didn't have that much vacation time only maybe five weeks altogether for the whole year and they were spread for summer, Christmas, and Easter, so it was not really like a university where one would have summer vacation two or three months.

It was during this summer that Cassie went for the first time to her church in Salzburg. The first three persons she met were three ladies. She said, "Good morning," and introduced herself by her first name.

Smiling, extending their hands for a gracious welcome the ladies asked, "Are you from Germany?"

When Cassie answered, "No, I'm not." They apparently were expecting that she was going to say, "Yes." She could just read it in their eyes. Then she said, "No, I'm not from Germany. I'm from Yugoslavia." Immediately their faces changed and she could see a very negative attitude something like, "Oh, no, we don't want to have anything to do with such people!" This was the first time that she really faced this enmity toward Eastern Europeans or Yugoslavians in Austria.

While she was in the Austrian schools there were so many foreigners there that she really didn't feel this enmity that much but now, suddenly, she was facing it very strongly and it was not in the school; it was not in the street; it was in the middle of her own church and she was just—"Puff!" completely blown away. At first they had seemed to have a faith like you couldn't believe then they turned around and left her standing there. She was shocked like, "What's going on?"

During the three years she spent in nursing school these three ladies never, ever greeted her anymore—she was really rather shocked but she still tried to think, "Okay I'm going to try my best." It was very common in Europe to have Youth Hour every church afternoon or evening so she went to this one in the afternoon and again she faced a young girl who asked her the same questions and she got the same reaction.

Cassie felt like her self-esteem was really dropping down very rapidly, but there was a bright spot there—Otto was a very young brother a little bit older than she was. He was a physical therapist and was very nice to her. He was a rather skinny guy with bluish-green eyes. Otto had this special genuine Christian love; he was really interested in being her friend and she really appreciated him. But of course at that point she was not really interested in any kind of special friendship because she just came out of a relationship with her German fiance and she was not really interested in anything other than having a friend, but she really liked him a great deal. He was just something special and she was thinking if it's God's will maybe later but not now. He would always try to go with her from the church to the dorm where she was living which was probably a 25-minutes walk and they really had a nice time just being friends.

About the time when she started nursing school there in 1991 one day she noticed nervous eyes behind newspapers glued to the headlines. Anxious voices exclaimed, "There's war in Bosnia." Stunned Cassie quickly looked over their shoulders. Her mouth flew open in awe as she saw the headlines—the newspaper headlines that were breaking the news all over the world that war in Bosnia had started. It spread from Sylvania over Croatia to Bosnia. The news brought great fear to Cassie. Her brow knitted as she gasped, "I wonder what is happening to my grandparents!" She tried to contact them but it was very agonizing to discover that her grandparents had to leave and nobody knew where they were! She really, really went through terrible agony as she heard of so many atrocities that were happening in that part of the world and wondering where her grandparents were.

Serious breaches of the Geneva Convention that was set up so many years ago in 1949 now occurred. Attacks were widespread against the civilian population. Bosian Muslim and Bosnian Croat civilians were persecuted on religious, national, or political grounds. Thousands were rounded up in internment camps to await acts of psychological and physical abuse and had to endure inhumane conditions. Many were killed or seriously injured.

People were tortured, murdered, raped, robbed, beaten, sexually assaulted. Political leaders, professionals, and intellectuals were fair game. Personal property of home and/or businesses were plundered or destroyed.

Women, children, and the elderly were detained and brutally treated in these internment camps. Girls and women were raped at the camps or taken to other locations and raped. Starvation rations were inadequate. Medical care was insufficient or non-existent.

Where would Cassie, a young girl with "mixed blood," be in this blood bath if only she hadn't been given that dream that she should leave the university. What if she hadn't have taken this dream seriously? Would she be put on the Bosnian Croat side since she mainly lived with her Croatian grandparents? What an unbelievable dilemma!

In the detention camps jewelry, money, watches and other valuables were stolen.

Weapons of mortar, rocket, and artillery were used by the Serbs to shell the civilians which weren't even of any military significance. Banja Luka saw near total destruction of some sacred sites.

UN peacekeepers were selected as hostages to use as "human shields" at places thought to be potential locations of NATO air strikes. The UN hostages were photographed by high level Bosnian Serbs showing them handcuffed at ammunition bunkers at Jahorinski Potok. Srebrenica was described as the worst place in Europe in the 20th century because of these crimes. It became the international community's greatest shame for not putting a stop to this horror. Mass graves have been discovered containing Bosnian Muslim, Bosnian Croats and Orthodox Serbs killed during this war

Many years later, in 2005, at a memorial ceremony relatives and friends wandered among hundreds of caskets of newly identified remains. These caskets were passed from person to person toward graves where they were given a descent burial. It was a memorial of weeping, along with the sound of shovels of dirt covering caskets as a loud voice read the names of the dead. Thankfully Cassie was not one of these!

God was watching over Cassie and her grandparents with His great love.

"My dream! That special dream with the dragon ready to devour me and the angel warning me, 'Cassie, you must leave this university. If you don't leave it's going to be disaster for you.'" Suddenly it dawned on Cassie the true meaning of her warning dream! She was of mixed blood. There was a real bloodbath of "ethnic cleansing" about to happen. She would have been one of the ones being especially targeted! Had she not been committed to God—had she stayed behind, being of "mixed blood" she was bound for the bloodbath—the real bloodbath of "ethic cleansing"!

This war in Bosnia was not just a skirmish between groups—a skirmish that was here today and gone tomorrow! It was not a war that just involved her countrymen. A full-blown war was going on, it's fires leaping at the heels of unexpected victims that were going about their daily affairs as usual. No matter whether you were a Serb or a Croatian, you could not feel safe but if you were born a child with a parent being a Serb and another parent being a Croatian you were of "mixed blood" and a special target to get rid of so that the world would only have a certain breed. It reminded the world of Hitler's reign when only those of certain characteristics were allowed to live. It seemed your looks, and not your character was the main thing that mattered.

Being a serious student Cassie thought back to her studies and remembered that it was an event in her very own country that had sparked World War I.

On a Sunday, June 28, 1914, shortly before noon crowds gathered in Sarajevo, the capital of the Austrian province of Bosnia. They waited eagerly to see the heir to the throne of Austria-Hungary, Archduke Francis Ferdinand, and his wife Sophie. Suddenly before their very own eyes a man jumped on the running board of the open-topped royal touring car where Ferdinand and his wife were waving at the crowd. The man fired a pistol. Shots rang out that started World War I. As Sophie tried to shield her husband from the shots she was hit by one bullet while two shots hit Ferdinand killing them almost instantly.

The assassin was a young revolutionary Bosnian student who had lived in Serbia. Austria-Hungary suspected that Serbia had approved the plot to kill Ferdinand. As the murder trial of the assassin was being arranged different countries sided with either the Serbs or Austria-Hungary. The turmoil that followed from the sides taking part brought on World War I that lasted from June 28, 1914 through November 11, 1918.

Cassie, now studying in Austria felt she was really doing well in school. She was one of the best students and was grateful for that but she was very discouraged because of the treatment she received in the church and had to say in the school itself maybe there were some people who were against the foreigners but she really couldn't feel it that strongly. But in the church the feeling was just so strong—it was so hard because church was everything for her, like family. And now suddenly she could forget this church; she was getting depressed and didn't want to go to church any more. She felt guilty because she knew she should go but she didn't want to be there.

In Austria it's not like the States where you can have several churches to choose from, if you don't like one you can go to twenty other ones close by. That was the only one, there was another but she didn't know where and since she didn't have a car it was just so far no one would drive that far so she started skipping church. In addition to this disappointment the news came about the war starting in Bosnia and her grandparents disappearing.

Cassie was totally devastated but every day she remembered her dream that she had three years before about the dragon that stopped the studies in Bosnia. She realized, "Wow, the Lord knew what was going to come and He protected me the way that He showed me in the dream that I should leave and be safe in this country!" She was so very grateful! Now it came to her very, very obviously why she had to leave the country. God loved her so much that He just wanted her to be safe. She was so grateful for that but she was also worrying about her grandparents.

She went to the Red Cross desperately trying to find her grandparents—she couldn't hear anything about them and it was really, really hard! Now was a time when she could have really been helped by the members of her church. Then suddenly after two weeks she heard that her grandparents were in a kind of camp for refugees in Croatia. They had been able to flee from their house.

Later she heard that the Serbs came to her grandparents' house.

Shots rang out down in front of their home. Grandfather peered out the window and saw a child crumble to the ground.

With no thoughts of himself and his own safety he only ran to try to help the child. As he leaned over the child who lay in a pool of blood he felt no pulse—the child lay dead. The sight of his lifeless body seared another memory of agony into a kind grandfather's heart!

Cassie's grandparents were Croatians in Bosnia. The village where they lived was a Croatian village. It was very common in Yugoslavia that villages mostly were either Moslem, Croatian, or Serb villages. During the communism years they were quite happily living together but now the villages were breaking up into quarters for different ethnic groups while the cities and towns seemed to be mixed together and to not have so many different ethnic groups.

In the villages since there were different quarters this little boy who was a Croatian boy was now killed by the Serbs. At the moment Grandfather leaned over the young boy the soldiers pointed their guns at him and yelled, "You old man, you better go into the house before you're dead yourself."

With a sinking heart Grandfather Ivan looked up to see the Serb soldiers pointing guns at him and demanding, "We want you to sign papers that you're leaving this house and everything in the hands of the Serbs and that you don't want it anymore, that you're not going to come back anymore. If you don't sign these papers you're going to be dead!" Grandma peered from the window and caught her breath as she saw the soldiers point their guns at her husband! They made it clear to her grandparents that they didn't have any other choice but to sign the papers if they wanted to live. The grandparents were stunned, completely drained, so drained that they could hardly move.

With the Serb soldiers overseeing all that Grandma and Grandpa did they could not really discuss their dilema.

The grandparents were able to hurriedly grab a few of their belongings—they were allowed only to take a bag in each hand; within a few minutes they left the rest of their belongings behind.

Grandpa Ivan and Grandma were put on a bus with other people crammed together, not knowing what would really happen next. How they were hoping and praying that they could get to neutral territory without being killed!

Very often the Serbs would put the Croatians or Moslems on the buses to leave for Croatia and tell them, "You know you are now on the way to Croatia as refugees," but in the middle of the way some other Serbian soldiers stopped them and told them to get out of the bus. Then sometimes they would ruthlessly kill all of them. So Cassie's grandparents were in this kind of convoy hoping to get to the neutral area alive where NATO was, and then get to Croatia where these refugee camps were.

Sure enough while they were still in the bus some Serbs stopped them on the way and demanded that they get out. Waving their guns at their captives the soldiers demanded that they had to leave the bus at once! Shots rang out as people crumpled to the ground around them—killed! All looked on in horror, hearts beating rapidly, feeling for sure that they would be the ones to be shot next—but finally the shooting ceased and fortunately Cassie's grandparents were left alive along with some other people. The victims would have to walk as quickly as possible until they reached the Croatian line.

Hearts pounding, legs pumping up and down as fast as they could go—they seemed to be going nowhere fast. Now they were trying to cross this neutral area as fast as possible in order to reach the Croatian line where they hoped to find security.

Going through the neutral area was really terrible knowing that the Serbians could shoot them from their line. What a frightening experience to know that even while they were almost to reach safety they could be shot in the back and life would be all over! Each step that they took brought them that much closer to home.

Some others with babies struggled to try to reach safety. The grandparents helped them carry those kids; while they tried to hurry as fast as they could; it was so depressing. Feeling their age, they still weren't going to let those kids be killed. Finally their toes reached the Croatian line.

The blessed thing was that Cassie's grandfather had a half sister and a half brother in Croatia who would give them a guarantee that they were going to take care of them. Because of these relatives they were able to enter into the Croatian territory. But many other people who didn't have anyone to give them a guarantee were sent back. They were not allowed to enter the Croatian territory because there was no guarantee from family or friends to take care of them.

Cassie was just so grateful that God provided His blessing that her grandparents were able to spend some time with the half sister and half brother there to try to start a new life.

At that point Cassie's grandparents were in their mid-sixties. She would hear that soon her grandfather had a heart attack; when they brought him to the doctor, the doctor could see that he had had some old heart attacks. She felt so sad for her grandparents who in their old age had to leave everything and had to try to start a new life.

It was so depressing to Cassie; she would skip church more and more and would start eating more and more, gaining more weight, and then would ask herself, "What is going to happen?" She was so happy that her grandparents had survived the worst but it was hard not to be able to see her Sunshine. She felt increasingly and slowly out of touch not only from not getting the fellowship from those in the church but from watching these things that were happening on the outside as ethnic groups from Yugoslavia and other Eastern European countries were fighting.

Now many were not welcome in Austria and some of the surrounding countries; it was a frightening experience to see her world falling apart. She could not help but wonder how safe it really was for her to be there, and how safe it really was for other people to try to help their neighbors. What was the future going to bring?

While it was really a struggle, Cassie was still continuing nursing school and doing really well but she was being all torn apart. Some of the people in Austria who were trying to be helpful to the people of Eastern European countries were underhandedly being persecuted, like one person who tried to help received a package in the mail and when he opened it a bomb went off and he lost his fingers; there were many accounts going around about this sort of thing happening.

One experience made Cassie really think! Quite often she had to go to extend her Visa at a special foreign place in the city. The way it was organized was that she had to come with her papers there. So many foreigners would come to that office that the office would need to open at 8:00 a.m. But if you would come at 8:00 the line would be so long that they would not take you. She decided to come at 5:00 a.m. so she could be first in line. When she came at 5:00 the line was so long again, like fifty people in front of her and many more were coming. All she could do would be wait and wait for her turn. She asked some of them when they came and they said 2:00 a.m. Because she was in school and couldn't wait so long, she started coming at 2:00 a.m. Even so, she would be like third in line instead of first in line.

Cassie didn't remember praying so much as she did one night while waiting third in line with at least a hundred and fifty people behind her. All this crowd were like animals running to this building and pushing each other. It was just terrible, and then finally they would get inside the building in the waiting room outside the front office, packed like sardines, squeezed next to each other. It was hard to even breathe. They would wait half an hour—squeezed together.

At that point they started giving tickets, like #1. In order to give out the tickets they had to open the door. When the door opened, suddenly the two in front of Cassie were behind the door and she was in front. The two thought she was going to take the #1 ticket and they slapped Cassie in the face as hard as they could. The soldier inside just ignored it all. Even though Cassie's face stung like fire and the tears were burning her eyes, the hurt was mostly in her heart. Her heart cried out, "Lord, how long am I going to be treated like an animal!" She didn't realize what danger she put herself in when the prostitutes were marching up and down. The Lord had such protection over her that she couldn't even describe it during that one year when she had to constantly go to get her Visa updated. It was a very traumatic experience!

Chapter 9

GRADUATION! MORE SURPRISES!

Cassie was all excited. Her graduation day had finally arrived. She'd worked diligently in her classes; she'd absorbed all she could to remember for her future career. She'd eagerly tended to her practical work on the hospital floors. Sometimes the constant answering of patients' lights, walking the long corridors from one room to another had been very tiring as it is for all nurses but the idea that she was helping others at a bad time in their lives had kept a smile on her face.

She had bonded with her other classmates—they would miss each other—they would miss this place but it had been a great deal of hard work to get to this point and they breathed a sigh of relief. Tonight would be graduation night.

The girls fixed each other's hair into special styles for the night.

As Cassie marched down the aisle in her special graduation gown there were no relatives to show how proud they were for her. She knew if Grandpa Ivan could have come that he would. She knew that the Sunshine of her life would be thinking of her especially on this graduation day! She reflected his smile as she marched in perfect stride. She was marching for him, too. She could only hope that he could fully realize all the support in many ways he had given to her, not only financially, but more importantly to give her a little nudge and a little pull to show her that she could succeed! His staunch determination that she would be able to leave the street kids behind, and to give her the confidence to see beyond her mom's troubles at that time had paid off! She'd turned out to be a "good apple" afterall—not only a good apple but the cream of the crop!

Cassie listened attentively to the address that was given at her graduation. She nodded with approval at the success after the hard work. She smiled with joy that she knew secrets that had kept her from being just a body that day on the railroad tracks! She rejoiced that God had made Himself real to her that day and had shown His love and protection in so many ways! He had helped her to truly become Somebody!

Saying good-by to her classmates was not easy. There were tears among them but they'd gone through school often bearing one another's struggles. Many did not have grandparents and other relatives that were suffering under the heavy burdens that Cassie's grandparents were but they tried to be of help as they were hearing about the atrocious situations in nearby countries.

Cassie was happy to be able to have a job in a hospital where she worked with maternity patients and newborns! It was a nice 800-bed hospital in the Alps out in the country. She had a little apartment of one and a half rooms just across from the hospital. She either rode a bicycle or walked to work. It was very common to ride bikes. There was good public transportation by bus if you needed to go into town. Of course it was a challenge biking up and down the mountains. But it was a nice job that she enjoyed. The fresh air, sunshine, and beautiful scenery was very special. The only disadvantage was the war conflict in Yugoslavia and the many refugees and fighting among each other.

Because Cassie had Serbian blood in her and carried her Serbian father's name since the Serbs were the "bad ones" she felt discriminated against and would not have her name on her door or mailbox. She was especially frightened one day when she heard that the lady in the apartment below her had someone destroy her car and her apartment—someone from another ethnic group! She was afraid she would come home to find her apartment torn apart and destroyed. She might be the next victim. Many letter bombs targeted some people including people in the post office, some TV anchormen and even the mayor in Vienna, who were basically trying to support refugees. These incidents hightened concerns.

In light of all these things that were happening Cassie decided it might be well to be a nurse in Africa or some third world country. She started to gather information about where she might go. At the same time she met a nice Austrian nurse that lived in the apartment next to her who had just come over from the United States. He was full of praises about the U.S.A.

Cassie applied to work for one year as a nanny in the United States. But under the circumstances she hardly dared believe that she would get a Visa.

Amazingly, she received word from the agency in two or three days in December of 1996 that she was permitted to have her Visa! God was watching over His daughter.

This was something that Cassie had dreamed of for many years but really didn't expect to happen—it was a wonderful surprise to her. She could hardly believe she was headed for America!

Chapter 10
A FLIGHT TO THE LAND OF THE FREE

In a daze (was it really true?) it didn't take long to gather her few belongings and pack her luggage. Sleep didn't come readily that night—she was simply too excited. Finally when she did fall asleep, it seemed almost the minute she lay her head on her pillow that the alarm clock was going off. Friends took her to the airport; they all gathered around, their arms around each other with a special prayer of safety and thanksgiving for her.

Fortunately, she got a seat next to a window and waved to her friends for the last time. Then the pilot spoke and the stewardesses cautioned them to put their seat belts on and explained where the bags were in case someone became airsick. Before she knew it Cassie was up in the air watching Austria go further and further away. What a panorama—the patchwork farms below and the fluffy clouds like cotton candy surrounding her. By the time she was over the ocean she was as comfortable as sitting in her living room conversing with her seat mate.

In January 1997, Cassie arrived in Washington D.C. on her birthday! It was her first day in a new country! She was totally alone and barely spoke, wondering what would happen next. The next weekend would be a training session for nannies in Washington D.C. This was an exchange program; nannies from the United States would go to European countries. Special agents provided this visitor exchange. The nannies would learn different languages, would help with kids, and would be given money so they could travel around.

After the long flight Cassie stood in the doorway ready to disembark. Her eyes took in new sights. From the busy airport she could see huge buses driving down the highways looking much bigger than the European buses. Other nannies now embarked to various other locations. Some flew to California, to Florida, or to Chicago. Cassie went to Long Island, in the country, away from the big city. The choice was made before she came to the United States. Pictures had been sent to her in Austria of the family members for whom she would work. She had stared at those pictures so many times until she had a mental picture of who would be picking her up.

As Mr. Wilson and his four-year-old son waited for their "nanny" to file out of the plane little Barry's eyes were taking in everything. He excitedly pointed at the big airplane circling and coming to a landing.

"That's Cassie's plane. See it coming down the runway!" Mr. Wilson tried to increase his son's ever-increasing vocabulary even with this singular visit to the airport.

Then as the line of weary passengers came closer to them he picked out Cassie from the picture they'd been given.

They searched each face as she came down the hallway—and their eyes caught.

"There's Cassie! See Cassie!" Mr. Wilson pointed to a smiling Cassie.

Cassie held out her hand for a warm handshake and gave Barry a little squeeze. Mr. Wilson carried Cassie's luggage to the car while Barry held her hand. All the way home they chatted about the trip and Barry pointed out things along the way that he was familiar with.

As they drove through the traffic of New York City, at times there would be a sudden stop as a rack of garments was being wheeled across the traffic—the one pushing the rack seemed to take it for granted that traffic would stop and he looked straight ahead, thinking of other things besides getting run over.

The crowds of people walked around a man, looking very pale, lying on the sidewalk. Was he dead or just drunk? No one seemed to even care—to them it was a common sight. But to a visitor it was a picture of distress.

Big semi trucks were parked in the streets; there was no other place to unload their deliveries. The streets had been laid out many long years before and the unloading situation had not been taken into consideration for this day and age. Horns were blowing. In the din of noise and heavy traffic there was a general mood of rudeness, but once in awhile thoughtfulness intermingled like at one point where traffic had come to a full stop when a milk truck stopped beside them, the driver seeing the little boy in the car, came to the window with a small carton of chocolate milk for Barry. Barry's eyes sparkled brightly as he took the drink and the driver wished them a good day.

Noise was everywhere, not just from the traffic. Every few minutes a big jet would thunder close overhead, or a police car, an ambulance, or fire truck siren would wail.

As the car came to a traffic light sometimes the light would be on the corner of a sidewalk—sometimes the light would be hanging over the middle of an intersection. If you lived here you got to know where the light would be but for a visitor this could be a big problem. And if the visitor wouldn't stop when it should there would be some guy wagging his finger at the bewildered driver as if he were a stupid moron.

Eventually they wound their way to the long underwater tunnel. When you lived on Long Island you felt like you were in a bottle—the only way you could get back and forth from the city to the island was to go in that underwater tunnel again.

Once in awhile there would be a trickle of water running down the tunnel wall and you'd wonder, "Could this thing ever come tumbling down!" It was a big relief when you reached the other end and your wheels rolled on solid ground again.

Amazingly when you left the big city behind only a few short miles away Long Island had some rather quiet suburbs.

As they travelled down the highway, at each stop Cassie wondered if this was "home." She was very happy and excited and ready for adventure. It was a really nice mid-class neighborhood in the small village of Huntington. It was safe and clean.

"Well, we're here—this is our home." Mr. Wilson opened the car door for Cassie

Barry ran through the door showing Cassie all the toys and his little brothers and sister and the dog. Mrs. Wilson laughed, "Slow down, Barry!" She gave Cassie a warm hug. They showed Cassie to her room and unloaded her luggage.

Mrs. Wilson had made a light lunch which was eagerly devoured, as little voices all tried to talk at once.

It would have been very difficult for any mother to care for twins alone, but to have another child at two years of age and yet another at four years of age—four little ones all under the age of four, it could be overwhelming. Not only wanting to be the very best dedicated mother but to be a university professor trying to be the very best professor—what a challenge! No wonder they needed a nanny—it would take a very special nanny to take this kind of responsibility. When they read that Cassie had her RN degree and worked in the pediatric department they felt she would be a special nanny.

Cassie felt comfortable and happy working for the Wilsons. The Wilsons were a very kind, understanding, loving family,

As the days went by the kids would teach Cassie the games they knew. They played "Patty Cake, Patty Cake Baker Man" with the little twins and wiggled the babies' little toes as they sang, "This Little Piggy Went to Market!" The twins giggled. And then Cassie would show them how to play some of the games she grew up with way over in Bosnia. She would tell them bedtime stories like her grandmother told her so long ago. The little ones would beg her to hide them like in a sink, covered with a dish towel or some other strange place for Hide and Seek.

My! Cassie hadn't seen so many toys! But there was not much time to play games.

During the year she was there Cassie got to watch them really grow! It was teething time for the twins. As usual during teething time these two little babies could get irritable as their little gums hurt from the sharp teeth trying to come through. Their little bottoms at this same time could easily get rashes from the acids in their bodies as they began teething. This was an especially critical time to keep them dry and to apply creams to keep the rashes away. It was a constant round of changing diapers on the twins. Keeping little heads shampooed to keep "cradle cap" from forming on their tender little heads also kept Cassie busy. Trimming tiny nails to keep them from scratching themselves could be quite a chore, also. Then when bedtime came there would be four little ones to get into their bedclothes.

Soon the twins were crawling all over the place. She was there long enough to see them take their first baby steps and watch them on their first baby walk.

The two-year-old barely had started his potty training when she had come. Cassie would be there to help her get her training pants down fast, to smile when things went well and smile when accidents happened. She tied their sun bonnets on in warm weather and helped them with their mittens and boots when the cold winds blew. She was nurse when the colds came and there were fevers and dirty noses to wipe.

Their little sticky kisses, tight hugs and "I wuv ou's" made it worth it all!

The Wilsons were a very kind, understanding, loving family. Cassie felt really comfortable and happy but as could be expected many times overwhelmed with so many kids. It was surely understandable that they needed a nanny and Cassie was so very thankful that they did. She wanted to take a vacation to see the many sights in the United States but was very responsible and still was needed to help and that's just what she wanted to do the most. During these months that Cassie stayed with this lovely family they let her use their car. She had a driving license before she came to the United States.

One thing that really touched Cassie's heart was that the Wilsons let her use their car without any question. When her mother had bought a new car in Germany and had come to visit Cassie, Cassie had asked if she could drive the car a little bit but her mother would not allow her to drive the car. Now she came to another country and they offered to let her use their car—it was amazing!

At first, when Cassie came to live with the Wilsons she really didn't know what to expect. She was shy and cautious but with time she learned that these kids were just wonderful, loving kids. The mother of this family was a university professor. The father worked in a village 10-15 minutes away. They usually left about 8:00 in the morning and stayed until 5:15–5:30 in the afternoon. When the father came home Cassie was basically free to go where she wanted to. Sometimes she stayed to help him. It was nice that she had her own room.

Soon Cassie got braver and travelled on the northeast coast to take English classes. In fact, she had several classes spread out over the months. She was just learning for the first time in her life that it didn't matter from what ethnic group she was. For months she didn't want to tell where she came from but she learned that it was okay—that she would not be ridiculed.

As the nanny time drew closer and closer to its end and Cassie read and heard the constant news of the atrocities that were escalating in her homeland she prayed so earnestly that she would not have to go back into the bloodbath that most certainly awaited her especially with her "mixed blood."

Before Cassie left Austria she was given a list of institutions in the U.S.A. that taught natural remedies. Cassie was very interested in adding these remedies to her nursing career. There was one of those institutions that had a hospital. This sounded appealing to Cassie to be able to work in this hospital while learning the natural remedies. It was advertised that it was a place where foreign students could work as they learned. She called this school to find out more information and liked what she heard. They worked with students to help get their Visa needs taken care of.

Cassie was also ready to socialize more with young people of her own age.

After these great months as nanny for the Wilson family and her Visa was running out it was time to move on, but the goodbyes would not be easy. Cassie thanked the Wilson family profusely for the great opportunity they had provided for her. In her heart she knew it was providential that she had been given this special chance to come to America if even for a few short months but she did not know the full extent of this big step to her future.

Cassie gave each little one a special long hug. They wrapped their little arms around their "nanny" and gave her little kisses. At their age they couldn't fully realize the separation for someone that they'd grown to love. For them time would go on. They would be with other nannies; there would be many new adventures. Mom and Dad would hold the family together. For Cassie, there had been no family to hold her securely—for her, life had seemed to always be full of moves; for her the future was unsure. When would she finally be able to rest in peace? That miraculous day when she was twelve and called upon God—if there really was a real God, to proclaim Himself someway somehow, to save her, to take the suicidal thoughts away and to help her to become "Somebody" was the beginning of peace in her heart. Were it not for His miraculous answer she would not be alive today. She would call upon Him now to guide her steps knowing that He would make all things beautiful in His time.

Chapter 11
ROLLING ON TO OTHER DREAMS

As the big bus made it's way to her next destination her eyes took in the beauty of America from its majestic mountains, fruited plains and rolling grains. She had many beautiful spots in her own country but of course it was much smaller than the United States.

As Cassie rode mile after mile going west, she took in the sights of many states. Breaking loose from the constant bumper-to-bumper traffic of the eastern coast, and the smell of the big oil tanks that hugged the sides of the freeway outside New York City it was beautiful to get out on the highway with less and less traffic and fresher air.

As the miles went by she grew tired but didn't dare drift to sleep. She wanted to see all she could see—to feel all she could feel of this blessed freedom. There were no boundaries, no checkpoints, no custom offices from state-to-state. It was unbelievable!

Shenendoah Valley was beautiful! So peaceful! There were many stretches of grass and trees, a house and barn in the distance, cattle on the hills, horses peaceably grazing or galloping with the wind—ribbons of tails sailing behind. There were lakes with here and there a fisherman in a nook. The bus rolled on around a town now and then.

Finally, the bus hissed to a stop in the city of her destination. The driver of the van from the hospital where she would learn and work caught her eye. He was a cheery, thoughtful, helpful person. As they rode the few miles to the hospital Cassie was impressed. It was a beautiful setting among hills of evergreens and broad-leaf forests. The life-style center where many people came to learn natural remedies was laid out in a tasteful way. Every room led out through it's own sliding glass door to the outside where fresh air and sunshine awaited. There were trails through the woods to get invigorating exercises. Cassie met many students from other countries who also had come to get this training. She made many new friends. The doctors, teachers, and staff were very gifted and made their classes very interesting.

Cassie roomed with other girls in a house that had a large living room with a piano they could gather around and sing. There was a big kitchen where they could cook if they wished, and a big dinning room. But the whole institution had a big cafeteria where delicious, healthful meals were served.

The nurses at the hospital helped her to get her nurses uniforms. A special part of each session whether it be a massage treatment, a hydrotherapy treatment, etc., was to offer a special prayer that that particular simple treatment for this day might bring health and healing.

There would be diabetics who came, many of whom learned how to be weaned from insulin. However, the highly trained professional doctors through their tests, etc., could tell when there were certain ones for which insulin was a must and they would need to stay on their insulin but learn other ways to cut down medications.

People came to go to seminars that taught how to loose weight, or how to ease stress, etc. This institution had many thankful people leave it's halls with a whole new meaning of wellness.

There was also a studied effort to set aside TV's and newspapers that brought in elements of distress— to cut out the world of crime, hate, and ugliness and enjoy the beauties of today in God's way.

But knowing that on the other side of the world in her own country things were falling apart, the bloodbath was still continuing, naturally caused a great deal of anguish for Cassie. Her prayers were for dear Grandpa Ivan and Grandma.

What the future would hold for her very own life she had no way of knowing. But she could rely on God's promises that He would be with her, lead her beside the still waters, cause her to lie down in green pastures. He would go with her through the shadows and bring her into the sunlight. Every storm would have its rainbow. Her life was strictly in His hands. She prayed not to worry but to trust that He would give her the strength she needed. She knew that one of His promises was not to let us go through anything that we could not bear. He would be by our sides through it all.

Chapter 12

THE KING GRANTS HIS DAUGHTER'S WISHES

When Cassie was in her teens she was quite sickly, having colds during the winter almost without a break. She was overweight and pale and her eating habits were very poor. She would eat a lot of sweets and baked, greasy potatoes and hot dogs.

Yugoslavians eat a great deal of meat almost for every meal. The people would usually eat three meals a day with the biggest meal being at noon. For some reason Cassie ate a lot of sweets like six pieces of cake after lunch. In order to keep her weight down she would not eat for a week and then start all over again. She never liked meat and fish but would eat hot dogs and hamburgers. She loved French fries and of course sweets. At that point her family ate no whole wheat bread, only white bread, as white as snow.

For breakfast Cassie generally would eat white bread with butter, jam, and milk. And sometimes there would be French toast.

For lunch it would be very common that there would be meat with potato soup. Generally, in Europe there would be soup and then salad.

So she was born on cow's milk. A farmer would come every day with fresh milk; her mother would boil it. She was surprised that she didn't get allergies when she was a toddler. Cows milk would be mixed with sugar and white bread, cut in squares and dipped in milk.

In the evening there would be leftovers. The evening meal also might have grits—grits made with wheat, not corn. They might also serve soup.

If you would invite people for a meal and you didn't serve meat it would be like not offering a complete meal. You would be slighting your guests if you did not serve meat. Very typically, also, bread had to be served with every single meal—always, always.

All her life Cassie would love to read; it was the biggest blessing to have books to read. When she was sixteen one day in a book store she bought a health book which was written by a French/Jewish opera singer. She was describing how she had a car accident and became paralyzed and how the doctors gave up on her. At that point in her life while she was lying in the hospital not knowing what to do she was introduced to a special life-style without eating meat. Because she didn't have anything to lose she left off meat, used herbs, got fresh air, and exercised—slowly her condition started to improve until finally she could get out of bed and start her career.

Cassie was so impressed. She decided not to eat meat, which she didn't like anyway, so after reading that book she decided to become a vegetarian. The next day she was already a vegetarian to the surprise of her grandparents who became very serious, declaring that within six months she was going to die without eating meat. Her grandmother didn't cook, and wasn't interested in being a vegetarian.

Two years before Cassie decided to become a vegetarian she had read a book about diet; she was overwhelmed, but it was too early for her to decide to become a vegetarian. No one knew she was thinking of becoming a vegetarian. But when she was sixteen she was ready and decided to be persistent; it was easy because she didn't like meat but she didn't know how to cook and no one taught her. She, being made of the stubborn sort, stuck to it. She wanted so much to learn how to cook. She started taking baby steps but the Lord was leading.

When she was seventeen and became converted there were several vegetarians that she met. These were the first vegetarians she had ever met in her life. They encouraged her to eat only vegetarian food; she was very grateful when she realized she was not alone.

At eighteen when she went to Austria to school, they ate vegetarian food but still ate eggs and dairy products. Then again she went a step farther in her diet and learned how to cook; they had cooking classes.

Five years later, in Austria when she finished her nursing school she wanted to go a step further without eggs and milk. She thought it would be difficult because the food wouldn't look good and maybe even wouldn't taste good, it looked terrible. They were translating American English into German and used recipes that Americans used, like bagels; she saw pictures of bagels but didn't know what those things were. She tried her best but it was not happening. She kept praying to know more how to make dishes that looked good and tasted good and the Lord gave her the desire of her heart.

"What a Daddy I have!" she exclaimed when God gave her one more desire of her heart and she came to the States and she loved the food. She was on fire, so excited that she would get up at 5:00 a.m. and ask the cooks to show her how they made breakfast. She learned and practiced, she was so excited and wanted to work in the kitchen. She was always grateful for the experiences she now had and exclaiming in her heart, "What a blessing!"

At first she washed dishes but very soon the cook realized she wanted to cook, then she started making salads. She liked to decorate, it was like Christmas, it was very exciting. She now had a new desire, to teach people how to cook. She asked a person in charge of Life-style work if she would be allowed to give cooking lessons. A French lady, one of the nicest you ever would want to meet started giving cooking classes and then when Cassie felt she already had enough experience in the kitchen she decided to work in the Life-style section.

She had another big dream—to write nutritional articles and make up recipes. But she didn't know how to ask if she could do this since she was a "foreigner" and didn't have perfect English. Who was going to give her a chance! She talked to one of the secretaries that was helping with the health journal magazine if possibly she might do an article. The secretary was not really that optimistic, She said, "No, but let's see, God knows everything about it."

One day it was Thursday and she was looking forward to taking a vacation in the spring of 1999. Suddenly the secretary told her that the person who was supposed to write an article couldn't do it. Now they needed someone to do an article. What was she going to do? She needed the one-week vacation and the rest. But she stayed the whole week and worked all day long to get the article done and many recipes to go along with the article. She tried several times to get the recipes just like she wanted them. So she became a partner in writing further articles as well.

When she felt so insignificant, God read the desires of her heart and answered those desires to learn how to cook healthful recipes and now He helped her to write articles and recipes for the magazine. She even finished a third article.

But now Cassie had a third dream. She wanted to give lectures to the Life-style guests, people who came to this institution for a week of rest and recreation, listening to health lectures, etc. She was studying so much nutrition and was trying so hard to learn many things that she wanted to pass on to others. While giving cooking classes she wanted to give short lectures about an hour's length on nutrition. But the people who ran this institution felt you weren't supposed to step in to do something of a higher level on your own. You weren't supposed to ask, that would show you were not meek. You always had to be asked. So she wondered how she was going to do this. But "the Lord knew all about it." He would step in and give people the impressions to ask Cassie; her heart's desires were made possible.

Doubtfully, many of these staff members at this institute never realized they were answering the desires of one little lady who had come so far by faith. Certainly they didn't know about her prayer that rang out in that park in Bosnia when all hope was gone. That prayer asked God, if there really was a God, to please help her to become someone that could be used—not just an ordinary person from an insignificant spot in the world but to become someone special. God, who has promised to answer every sincere prayer we make to Him, must have looked down with special favor on this handmaiden of His. How the angels must have sung with supreme happiness as they helped to make her dreams come true.

One day the lady who was in charge of arranging for people to do the lectures came to her and asked her, "Cassie, would you be willing to give some of these lectures? I think you have this talent to do these lectures." She had to put on her meekest and most humble face, and if you were really a good Christian you had to say, "Let me pray about it." Of course she was almost to explode for happiness.

So she started lecturing. Most of the time she would go to the reference room and a couple of other places to do her studying. She read the writings of someone who said that we can only become fearful if we forget how God has led us in the past.

While she was in nursing school she realized she had this eating disorder. Because she didn't want to get too fat, she needed to eat less. She would take laxatives actually believing that this was the thing to do but she didn't know how harmful this really was. So after realizing she had this problem she started to read about it and then she knew something had to change—that she could bring damage to herself.

She wanted to vomit but couldn't get it up. It was a blessing that she was not able to vomit because now she read that this was one of the worst ways to get rid of food. It's a secret, sick disease. Everybody thinks they are so healthy but only you and God know something is wrong. This was actually in the first year of nursing school when she realized she had this problem and started to get help; she was spiritually so low; but she began to realize one can't think of spiritual things when you are so full of food, you actually get depressed.

Cassie was really addicted to sweets. It was sad but funny when she was nine or ten years old she went to visit her grandfather. Her grandparents had sold their house and now for the time being her grandfather had to stay in the city; he rented a room for a short period of time. Once Cassie went to visit him while he was renting a room; the owner was an old, old Moslem whose husband was like a Moslem priest. He died—now she was a widow. Because she was the priest's widow she always lived next to the Mosque to minister to the guests.

It was the time of the Ramadan feast and this widow made many typical Moslem types of desserts that were very rich. This day she baked these oval cookies on baking sheets, about a dozen cookies to a baking sheet. Cassie saw those cookies and wanted them. She took one cookie and moved the others so it didn't look like an empty space but she wanted one more and it still looked pretty, and then she wanted more and more until before she knew it she had eaten the whole sheet. Because she was the priest's wife this lady had made many sheets of these cookies so that the visitors could have something special.

Cassie knew she was in trouble, she had to do something fast so she went to her grandfather, "Grandfather, something terrible happened! I ate the whole sheet of cookies from the priest's wife!"

He exclaimed, "Oh, no! Cassie! Wow! What are we going to do? We'll have to go and buy some that's all I know to do." He then talked to the priest's wife and apologized and told her they were going to buy some from the bakery. Cassie was so worried; but the widow was so nice. She was laughing, "Don't worry we have plenty more." Cassie couldn't understand—no one could understand how she could eat so many sweets when she was at such a young age.

But when Cassie began the total vegetarian diet and started eating two meals a day her cravings for sweets got less and less but still she was often depressed. She thought she could eat like a whole bakery. When she was feeling good she would eat sweets only once a day and be happy.

Cassie began to realize that eating was very much related to her spiritual life. So with God's help, after many years she thought she got the victory but if she were not really strict with her eating—the eating disorder would come back. She thought she was worse than an alcoholic since you can live without alcohol but you cannot live without food. You are always exposed to food. Now every day she would ask that the Lord would help her to eat right.

While she was working in New York she went to Overeaters Anonymous and learned their 12-step program. She learned that eating disorders involved God—not just satisfying the mouth for the moment. God is in control; she had a good experience in New York where she did not have to go through this alone but learned from educated people who were really in the know.

Cassie, always eager to learn, was absorbing so many new things from this fine institution that was helping so many people with their health and healing. She would always thank the Lord for leading her to this exact place at this exact time in her experience in life.

Chapter 13
STRANGE COINCIDENCE

In December of 1998 Marie became very ill with a virus that was going around this particular winter. Even though she was so nauseated she couldn't eat very much and what little she ate came right back up, still her sugar went very high in spite of the insulin she was faithfully taking.

Being a person brought up in the era from the locale where you didn't go to the doctor unless you felt you were on your death bed, she was ill several days before she decided she'd better see the doctor.

Her regular internist was afraid she was becoming a "brittle diabetic," that maybe she was allergic to insulin. He frankly told her that he had done all he could do for her and wanted to turn her over to another doctor who had a great deal of experience working with diabetics. When he said the name of the doctor, she recognized it as being a doctor she had gone to before but had chosen another internist who was much closer to her home.

She was willing to travel the extra miles in order to get well. She was very happy to hear this familiar doctor's name. She repeated the name and wrote it down, with the internist by her side.

That night her fever soared. She was delirious and said things she never knew she was saying. One of the things her husband, Keith, heard her say was the clincher. He decided right then and there that she was going to the hospital. She moaned, "Jesus, I'm ready, just let me go!"

She had told her husband that her doctor wanted her to go to this other doctor so he called and the new doctor admitted her to the hospital. This hospital was a hospital that treated with natural means, as far as possible. She had very little strength left. The first day for breakfast it was all she could do to cut her apple. She was worn out under just that much exertion. Her sugar was high; her blood pressure was high. She was given a sed test which went over 100. For women the test results shouldn't have been over about 20, she was told. Clearly there was some infection other than any virus that was going around.

The doctor put her on two different types of insulin, a long lasting, slow type of insulin, as well as a faster type to take 3 times a day. She had hot and cold water treatments and fomentations. There was a big jug of mixed herbal teas for the high blood pressure as well as other herbal teas for infections. They were bitter, very bitter, especially since she was not able to sweeten them with a bit of sugar. The meals without sugar as well as without salt were very bland but she was here to get well. The atmosphere was so good. The students who were learning these natural ways of healing offered prayers, sincere, caring, beautiful prayers that God would use these simple treatments to bring healing according to His will.

All the regular staff and each student was really special but there was one student that especially impressed Marie. She had such a beautiful smile and winning, caring ways. She reminded Marie so much of her daughter. She spoke with a distinct accent. Keith spent many of the eleven-day stay days and nights sleeping on the floor beside her. The first time Cassie met him he surprised her by rising up from his floor pallet and peeking over the bed. Right away they learned she had a good sense of humor. When they asked what country she came from they learned she was born in Bosnia.

Several months before they'd volunteered to help a refugee family who had come to the States from Bosnia. Keith took turns driving the husband back and forth to work until he could get his own vehicle and licenses, etc. He helped to get doctors to give free examinations for the family and as they helped with different projects to help them get settled in this new country they became such special friends and seemed like part of their family.

As the days went by Cassie would walk down the hall with Marie as she gradually got her strength back and offered to go with her as she ventured to walk outside just in case her strength would give out.

After what seemed an eternity, the eleven days ended. Marie's diabetes was under control. She was getting her strength back and was ready to go back to work.

As the weeks went by they thought it would be nice to invite Cassie to their home and also thought it would be fun for her to meet this other Bosnia family, thinking that they would know each other's language and be able to communicate well. It was fun seeing these countrymen together. Little did they know until they heard in the news later that some members of refugee Bosnian families still were having difficulties with their sentiments against different ethnic groups even in this new land. They learned that they had just as soon choose their own groups of friends in this new land. They loved each family that they became acquainted with but respected their feelings toward each other.

Later when they called to see if Cassie could come for dinner and a visit at their home they were told that a few days before someone had called the lifecenter wanting them to call Cassie and tell her that her Visa had expired and that now she was on the deportation list. Now they said Cassie "took off" and might be visiting her friends in New York or California. The word had spread that she was "on the run." They were so sorry to hear this but hoped it wasn't true. They asked that if anyone heard from her or if she came back to please let her know that Keith and Marie were trying to work something out for her. Keith had already sent a letter to a congressman asking for his help.

They had been listening to the news—the gruesome things happening in Bosnia, especially the tragedies awaiting those of "mixed blood" those who were neither Serb, nor Croatian. They heard of groups that were taken into the woods, mutilated, raped, and often killed. Before their eyes they could almost imagine what would happen if Cassie had to go back. This could never happen to this beautiful, caring nurse. They were determined they would fight with tooth and nail, with every legal means they could muster to help Cassie be saved. They remembered Cassie in their every prayer. She had no idea what she meant to Keith and Marie. To this day they still don't think Cassie can ever realize their concern and love for her.

Finally, the day came when they received a call from Cassie! She was back at the medical institution where she had been a student. She had learned so much about the natural ways of healing. She had been especially impressed to come to this life-style center above other similar life-style centers about which she had heard. She was not "on the run." She had decided that if she had to leave that she would take this bus tour and be able to see the

USA before being deported—the beautiful country she had read about so long ago and that she had dreamed about visiting. She had told some of her friends at the center about this tour but the other rumors that she was on the run had prevailed. In reality, after being denied the extension of her Visa Cassie was just spending a month on a special tour on the Amtrack from Atlanta to California, Seattle, Chicago, Florida before she had to leave. It was a very stressful time for Cassie and she needed this trip as a special time of relaxation. Did she ever get to see the Yellowstone Park where she had dreamed about seeing those fun-loving bears she'd read about so long ago? No, the train didn't go to this stop. She would have to take a bus and it would be so much extra time—so near, but too far to see those bears. There were always different people on this train but Cassie was not afraid of these strangers. She felt the peace of God with her. She would sleep in youth hostiles that were cheap for back-packers. At last the trip came to an end. She knew she had only one thing to do and that was to now pack up her things and head back to her country and face whatever she had to face. When she arrived back at the center she had a letter from the congressman Keith had contacted. She felt that it was impossible and couldn't believe it could work. Later she believed God let all of them experience this so they could let God work out miracles. Without much hope and knowing she had her own troubles she didn't know if she should put much stock in this letter but she called Keith and Marie anyway.

They rejoiced to hear Cassie's voice again and went to pick her up for a visit to their home. She wanted to stay at the center and learn more and participate in studies there. Keith called the person in charge of this phase of student studies. The first words from the man at the center were stunning, "She is no longer welcome here!" What! This was a Christian institution (surely this one man did not correctly represent the thoughts and feelings of others in this Christian institution). They couldn't believe Christians could ever tell anyone, "You're no longer welcome here!" especially when she had done nothing to deserve this. So Keith started explaining what she'd been going through thinking she would be deported and tried to get the man to put himself in her position and see things as she saw them from her viewpoint.

As Marie sat beside Cassie and watched her brown eyes and the expressions on her face when Keith related what the man (now he'd put Keith on hold) had said, "She's no longer welcome here," Marie was amazed at the serenity of her face. For as long as Marie lives she will never forget Cassie's face at that moment. Marie would have been crushed. She would not have been able to keep the tears from falling, to be so unjustly thought of, it would have been a shock to her. Was it because she had heard so many things like this in her life that it was only second-nature now to accept them or was it a deep, inner faith that forgave people who said such remarks and knew as she would say so many times later, "God knows all about it." She was so serene, looking forward, as if she had never even heard the words, like a lamb waiting for the slaughter if it had to be. This was her attitude for many months while waiting in limbo.

Fortunately, by the time Keith had finished the phone conversation, God had impressed on the man to tell her she could come back; they would have a committee meeting to decide more details.

The people at the center, at the last minute, had tried to get an extension of her Visa, but for some reason hadn't given enough information; they gave up trying any more. But God was still fighting her battles and He worked with Keith and Marie as they did all they could to keep her here. They prayed for His directions in all their plans. Not only did God fight Cassie's battle for her to stay at the center but He made it possible for her dream to be able to cook these healthful recipes to come true. She not only learned to cook in this fashion but in such a short time she was teaching others how to cook. And then her dream of being able to give some of the lifestyle lectures came to pass. And then her dream to write articles for the lifestyle health journal came to pass. In one instance she was told she was no longer welcome and suddenly her talents were being used to enlighten others. God, who had intervened in her life so many times would still open the way for His daughter.

Although Cassie had a deep faith and trusted God with her very life still she was human and as such she couldn't help but try to guess what the outcome for her life would be.

Keith wrote the congressman again, who was very helpful. Keith arranged for TV coverage so that she could get letters of support from the community. One of the news anchormen had relatives back in Bosnia and wrote a great letter of support for Cassie.

Interestingly enough there were some men, young and old, who offered to marry her, some sight unseen. Although they probably were sincere in trying to help, Cassie was determined that when and if she would get married that it would only be to someone she really loved.

Keith arranged for the church they attended to write letters of support so that the government would know that she would not be a burden to society.

Cassie wrote a letter to the President; she was amazed when Keith told her she could go ahead and send this letter because in her country a common person wouldn't presume to do such a thing. Keith sent a letter of support along with her letter to the President. A few days later Keith would hear in the news of how the President's wife was supporting a group of Bosnian ladies and he also sent a letter to her.

When Keith called the only immigration attorney in their city; he finally agreed to speak with Keith for a few minutes. It ended up that they visited for about an hour and a half. Keith wanted to get Political Asylum for Cassie. The attorney held no hopes for her getting this asylum. Keith called Immigration and got the Political Asylum forms. Cassie filled out the forms; they waited and waited for a reply. Finally they got a letter telling Cassie and her representative to come for a meeting at the Immigration office in the big city about two hours away.

They stopped along the way to grab a bite to eat. Cassie didn't eat. Marie wondered why. Cassie had made some special goodies for them, some substantial whole wheat sandwiches, etc. It was so sweet of her and Marie eagerly munched her sandwich with a glass of milk. Keith, who didn't care for whole wheat bread, ordered something according to his tastes at a diner. Cassie didn't eat, didn't talk, and Marie wondered if they'd said or done something wrong. It took awhile for Cassie to learn to trust them. She had been on her own since she was thirteen and had to be cautious. It would not be for many months that Marie would discover what her silence meant and to know what she was really thinking. You see, in her country it would take much time to get to destinations and her grandfather would leave many hours ahead of time to get to an appointment. If you missed the time the appointment was made you lost that meeting—period. When they went to this big city it was a common thing that you never knew just how the traffic would proceed. In the heavy traffic, it was understandable if you got caught up in traffic, it was not an appointment that had to be on the dot. Now, many months later when she explained how it was in her family in another country Marie could understand how Cassie was on pins and needles, she would have been, too, were she in Cassie's situation.

When they arrived at the Immigration building Keith let them off while he went to park their vehicle. Marie had her camera, anxious to take Cassie's picture when she won her asylum (unaware that this was only the beginning of any procedures). But while going through the metal detector she was not permitted to take her camera inside; she was told to put it in the car. She tried to explain that she had no idea where their vehicle was and couldn't leave the camera there—what could she do?

Finally she placed the camera behind a poster in the corner but was quickly told she couldn't leave it there. She saw a janitor cleaning the steps outside and asked him if she could leave her camera behind a cigarette trash can—she appreciated his understanding as he lifted the top sand portion and let her put her camera concealed in the bottom of the stand. While all this was going on Cassie was off and running to her next stopping place. When Keith came Marie told him she was worried about where Cassie might be. He smiled and assured her Cassie was a world traveler and knew how to take care of herself. Sure enough Cassie soon joined them.

As they sat in this big room full of benches, Marie heard things she couldn't believe and saw things she never would have expected in a USA immigration office. She heard an officer angrily talking loudly to one man, for all to hear, "You knew you were expected to bring this (something he was trying to explain he thought another member of the family had brought)!" But because he had not brought it, he was told to go home that he had no hopes. Marie watched the man, bent with downcast eyes, each step down the aisle as if he were lost in a world of despair where no one cared; his destiny seemed to hang in the hands of one man, who seemed so heartless. She saw another person treated about the same. She wondered where our diplomacy was. Did we really have a heart—or was it just plain hard business? She saw the crushed look, the slumped shoulders in genuine anguish.

Many months later she listened to a documentary on TV from immigration officers and their plight as to how to meet their challenges. From this documentary she discovered that the opinions of the officer himself/herself had so very much to do with the decision as to whether a person got to stay or had to leave. Some officers were so stressed by the life and death decisions that they had to make that they decided to move on to other jobs—it was just too overhelming. Marie gained more appreciation for the officers who were dedicated to sincerely caring for others.

As Cassie's name was called two ladies came to the door to greet them. One counselor was helping another counselor who was not yet familiar with all the procedures. As they waited longer Marie sent up an earnest prayer that Cassie could have the counselor who was the most familiar with the circumstances.

When the door opened for Cassie to follow the counselor to another floor, to another room, they were disheartened to see that it was the new lady, the lady with less diplomacy as well. Keith, coming as her representative was not allowed to stay with Cassie. They waited outside the door praying that Cassie would understand the questions, etc. Then finally Keith was asked to come in. He was astounded that the lady knew so little about what was actually happening in Bosnia. He tried to help her understand the circumstances, that if Cassie were to have to go back that she would almost certainly be killed. More evidence was called for, more things on paper as to how she'd be harmed. What more evidence could you ask for, the newspapers, the TV were full of the atrocities happening every day! They couldn't understand how anyone could be immune to these news accounts. Keith tried to explain the real circumstances with such feeling that came from his soul that the counsellor finally turned to Cassie and said, "You've sure got someone to take care of you, don't you!" And then the meeting was over—Cassie and Keith came out the door. The counselor didn't seem to understand much about was happening in the far away country of Bosnia, and how much weight her words would carry. The next step would be that she would take these facts to a committee. All they could do was to pray that God would fight Cassie's fight—that He would help the new counsellor to speak the right words, the words that were so crucial—the words that could mean the difference between life and death.

On the way home Cassie was sick; she fell asleep, her head falling on Marie's shoulder. Was Cassie born to die young? Would she be sent back to the place where mixed blood was being spilt as if it were simply water?!

Cassie's life was like a feather adrift on a raging ocean. At any second this life could be sucked down into depths that were out of anyone's control. But would the Man that had stilled the angry waters see fit that her life would continue to be? It was all in His hands! All they could do would be to wait, trusting this life they had come to love, this life they so desperately had tried to save in the only simple ways they knew how that indeed this life would be saved. All they could do now would be to leave this life completely in His hands.

Amazingly enough—the doctor that Marie went to in this natural lifestyle center wasn't even the doctor that her other doctor had recommended, it was a similar name! Had she not have gotten so desperately ill—had she not gone to this particular hospital they would never have met Cassie! Thank you Jesus!

Cassie has been a special song in their lives—a song of faith, hope, courage, and love. They prayed so earnestly that she could stay—she was so brave—she had no assurance that she wouldn't be sent back but she trusted God to know what was best for her life. Each day, each week they waited for the INS decision; it seemed like an eternity.

When the answer came Keith brought the letter from the Post Office to Marie's work. They were choked with tears when they read she had been granted the asylum, almost too choked to talk when Cassie answered the phone. On the other end they heard this whoop of joy when she heard the news! Then Keith arranged for a follow-up on the TV channel at which time Cassie saw her letter in print for the first time. She beamed with great joy! They all rejoiced!

They celebrated by taking Cassie out to dinner and arranged for their florist to bring her a dozen red roses. The florist manager wanted to bring them to the dinner herself. She was so impressed that she also brought another dozen roses—this time of mixed colors. Cassie's face was aglow as they carried the two dozen roses out the door and people were saying, "How does she rate—I've never had *two* dozen roses!"

Later Cassie lived with them for a couple of months; they loved having her with them; they heard more of her experiences; they were overjoyed to have her presence in their home—it seemed like they were privileged to have a real live, unbelievable person of rare faith and royalty living in their humble home. They often said to each other, "Is she for real!"

Then one day she said she had something important to talk to them about and had them sit on the couch. Maybe they knew one day it would happen but it came as a big surprise. She said she had been looking for a little place for her to stay on her own and had found a neat little apartment.

For some reason they really couldn't understand, the hearts of both of them sank at the moment she was telling them this. Had they not been the right kind of people for which she wanted to live? They thought they had done everything to make her comfortable; they knew they loved having her in their home. They knew that when she got on her feet more financially that she would want her own home but they thought that would be several months before she went out on her own.

Cassie assured them that she really appreciated staying with them but she felt the Immigration would probably feel like she would be able to support herself completely if she had a home of her own. They didn't feel that way; they wanted her to know she was welcome to live with them as long as she wanted to. After the initial letdown of their feelings Marie remembered the sinking feeling when her own children went away to college and she realized it was probably the last time they would really be living at home. But then after the initial heartache she had to see that it was a joyful thing that now they would have their own homes, a thing they had tried to prepare them for all their lives. After all, hadn't she as a teen-ager looked forward to having her very own home with her own husband and children to come. It seemed there naturally would be a sadness to see them leave but in time it would be a pleasure to see them in their own homes.

Now Cassie was off on her own—and they had come to love her as much as if she were their own. It was like leaving the nest. They could now see that she was so very happy to have her own little apartment—her first home in America.

Then Cassie's papers for permanent USA residence came. Once again there were papers to fill out, to type up, health check-ups to take in a city about two hours away, and immunizations to take—along with the long wait again, feeling there was no chance for her to lose but knowing the pitfalls in this world, still trusting all in the hands of God.

When they see the wonder in Cassie's eyes—coming from a communist regime—at the churches on almost every corner, of the many schools in every town and village they realize for perhaps the very first time how fortunate they are even though, financially, they are from the middle class in America.

Marie will never forget the expression in Cassie's eyes when she first went to the big Wal-Mart supermarket where you can buy anything you need; she said she never saw anything like that in her country—and they never knew they had it so good! What an inspiration Cassie is!

Chapter 14
THANK YOU AMERICA!

Cassie wanted to write a letter to the President of the USA. When Keith assured her it was fine to do so, Cassie wrote:

I was born in ... 1971, in an ex-Yugoslavian city called Nis by a Serbian father and a Croatian mother. From a very early age I was confronted with the hatred between these two ethnic groups. At the age of five my parents finally got a divorce; I then went to Bosnia and Herzegovina to live with my maternal grandparents—who are Croatians, until I was 18.

The problems between different ethnic groups became worse and worse. I decided to leave the country and go to Austria where I first attended language school. When I started nursing school the war broke out and the whole world understandably had negative feelings toward Serbia—based on its aggressiveness. Very soon the country was divided and the Yugoslavian passport was not valued any more. Having a Croatian mother, growing up in the care of Croatian grandparents, and seeing the violence of Serbia (even in my own family when my grandparents had to leave their house and everything they owned and flee at the age of 70 to be refugees) I wanted to have a Croatian passport.

Very soon the Croatian embassy in Austria let me know that because of my Serbian father, and being born in Serbia the only chance maybe to get a Croatian passport would be to be baptized in a Catholic church; already being a member of a protestant church it was impossible for me to do this step, and I had to take the Serbian passport. I felt very much religiously persecuted.

Ethnic and social persecution, and physical threats followed. Many different refugees from former Yugoslavia were now in Austria and other Western and Northern European countries. I and many other countrymen got telephone calls with threatening messages from ex-Yugoslavians and Austrians.

One underground political party (a remanent of Hitler's party, that is working especially against foreigners) was very active and sent many letter bombs to different domestic and foreign individuals engaged in work with foreigners. Even the Major from Vienna lost some fingers through one of these letter bombs. The similar underground parties were becoming very active in Germany, Belgium, Netherlands, and other countries.

I was in a country where the people hated my ethnic background, and on the other side in my own country my mother's and my father's ethnic groups were killing each other. Each group wanted one ethnic clean country where there was no space for me.

I lived in fear. I didn't have my name on the door or mail box. I had to isolate socially so that nobody would ask me for my name and background. At work I had to listen to nasty jokes from some coworkers.

I became an RN but didn't see any future for me. Depression came into my life and the solution that I saw at that point was to commit suicide.

Only through a miracle from Heaven I came as an Au Paire to the USA January 1997. The guest family was wonderful, but I was still very anxious to socialize. As time went by I realized that the U.S. is something different. It is a melting pot of the world and you are respected for who you are. I started to feel human again, and thankfulness grew in my heart when I realized that there is a country in this world where I don't have to fear for my life.

After being an Au Paire for one year I applied for a R1 visa and started a 6-months course in preventive and natural medicine. The R1 visa was rejected and I saw myself already socially and economically persecuted, raped, and killed. Through encouragement from some friends I filed for Political Asylum in July 1999.

I have a dream. I don't have a dream to have millions in the bank, or a fancy house with a swimming pool. I have a dream to be treated as a human, no matter where I was born or what my parents are. I have a dream to see my children being born and growing up in a country where humanity is the principle. I have a dream to offer my children a place to live where they can be proud of—no fear, no more persecution.

Believing in a God who can do miracles is the foundation of my life today. It doesn't matter what kind of refuge you need, He is with you. Maybe you are sick and in pain, or your partner left you; maybe your child is dying, or you are suffering under an addiction. Maybe you have enough from this life, and want to do the last step, and go to rest. Miracles can happen in your life through Jesus Christ. Your angel is right now standing next to you, and the whole universe is praying that you can completely surrender your life to Jesus, and let Him do the same miracles that He did in the lives of Abraham, Joseph, Lot, Moses, and Daniel.

I went the journey from Hell to Heaven and can only say, "Thank You God, and America! GOD BLESS AMERICA!"

(Editor's Note: *This was written when the President of the USA was in deep trouble, going through a struggle that seemed insurmountable for his personal life as well as not being impeached. Did the President ever read this letter personally or did it only go to the assistants. If he did get to read this, personally, surely it must have given him hope. Was this a girl like Esther coming to the government "at a time such as this"? Maybe someone read—maybe someone's life was touched. Marie's was. Keith's was.*)

Chapter 15

CASSIE'S FIRST HOME IN AMERICA!

When Cassie rented a small apartment—her very first home in America, it was exciting for her. She counted her pennies carefully. She did not want to rely on others but wanted to be able to support herself. One day she was able to purchase a small, used, table and chair. She brought them home and scrubbed them until they looked almost like new. She found a lovely table scarf and a pretty centerpiece of candles and flowers. She bought a beautiful, but inexpensive set of china.

Cassie and Marie had some special times together as they sat and talked while she scrubbed her "new" furniture. She was having so much fun making her own "little nest." They felt they'd had a rare opportunity to have this "queen" in their presence, in their home and in their lives. What a lot of miracles Cassie has been through during her lifetime and she has so many wonderful years ahead of her.

Cassie talked of marriage but she'd recently thought that maybe she was meant to be single. Then she'd earnestly done some pondering. Maybe she'd been looking for the wrong type of guy, she wondered. Always before she was looking for the aggressive type of fellow—the king who would be the boss—to be the takeover type, the type of fellow going before and she'd just follow after.

After doing a great deal of analyzing on this subject, now more and more it seemed to her that she was the aggressive type of person. Maybe it would be better if she looked for the type of fellow who was happy to be on the more quiet side.

Cassie had spoken in all honesty that she and Grandpa Ivan were "determined" and sometimes "impatient" about getting things done. They'd make a way to do what they felt needed to be done.

Not long before getting her Political Asylum Cassie and a fellow around her age started being special friends. At the life-style center where she was learning about the natural remedies, it was felt that a couple should go through a friendship space before actually going out on dates with each other. Then, they should ask the parents or guardians for their permission before pairing off. And of course, they should definitely get their okay before becoming engaged.

So Cassie and Paul had fun working in the garden together or going for a walk down the exercises trails where many people walked. Paul was the son of some high officials at the life-style center and as they were seen more and more together people started nodding in approval thinking it might be a good match. Cassie enjoyed Paul's company and they became very good friends. But as the days went by Cassie could see that as far as marriage they were incompatible with each other. It wasn't easy, but one day Cassie decided she had to be fair and not give any hopes; he should be able to get on with his life and find that someone to fulfill his desires. She finally got up her courage and let Paul know in as best manner as she could that she would like to stay special friends but that she couldn't have a relationship that went any further than this.

Not too long after breaking up with Paul Cassie got her Political Asylum. She was so thankful that she broke up just when she did, otherwise it might have been easy for people to say she was just "using" Paul as a way to marry and get to stay in the U.S.A. At the time she broke up with Paul there was no hope for any way to get to stay in the U.S.A. The farthest thing from Cassie's mind was to marry someone just to get to stay in the Land of the Free. When she would get married it would be to someone she genuinely loved.

After moving to her own apartment Cassie started visiting a Spanish church near her new home. While visiting there she became acquainted with Dan whose parents were missionaries to South America. Cassie, always wanting to learn new languages enjoyed talking with Dan about his experiences in South America and she liked picking up and learning Spanish words.

Dan became a good friend. She spoke of feeling he really cared for her and she had some thoughts of becoming a closer friend to him. As time went by once again, she grew to realize it would only be a friendship.

Cassie decided to have a small group of friends come over to her home each Friday night to study the Bible. There were about five or six of them. It was fun to get together for inspirational thoughts and just to see each other after a busy week.

There was one fellow at Marie's work whom she had learned that his wife had died a couple of years before. Jeff seemed sad. She'd ask him, "How did your holiday go?" and he'd reply with a sad look, "Oh, I made it." He seemed to be quite lonely. He lived near Cassie and Marie told her about this fellow at work that lived close and wondered if it would be okay to invite him to the group. She thought it would be nice for him to get together and make friends. She never wanted to be a match-maker in any way. She'd long ago learned that you might think people would make a good couple but that it might turn out to be just the opposite. She didn't know Jeff very well at all, only that he was a good worker where she worked.

Cassie thought Jeff was a nice fellow and she greeted him each week as she did the others in the group as good friends

Each week Cassie was the leader of the group. She'd study during the week on a special topic—they'd open their Bibles and each read certain texts and add their thoughts as this text might have brought up different experiences in their lives.

Cassie longed to have a musical instrument for which someone would play since they'd start by singing some songs together, so she started praying for this. One day at work the lady said she had an electrical keyboard that she could have for $20.00. "Twenty dollars!" Cassie was overjoyed—it was like a miracle. She played the keyboard as they made a circle around her to sing. It became a special part of the weekly group to sing gospel songs together.

Cassie had made a list of traits she'd like to see in the type of husband she'd like to have.

"Well, when you find this kind of person you let me know. I'll get a chain and put him in a cage and hold him for you. This type of person is really going to be almost impossible to find!" Keith chuckled but also felt this would indeed be a rare person to find.

As the list progressed Cassie then decided that there were certain things that were a must but that since they were two completely different individuals that each should have their preferences on certain things and not compel each other to do just as they wanted them to do.

She wanted someone that was of her faith, that was a must to her. There are so many things that can keep a couple from seeing eye-to-eye but with this foundation of belief together and coming to God in prayer in one accord was most important, she felt.

Then there were other things on her list that would be nice to be together on, but she realized she could still live with that. It would not HAVE TO BE.

One of the things at the top of her list would be that he would not be so intent on watching TV that it would take away from their togetherness with other priorities.

She hoped that he would not be so wrapped up in sports that they would be his main emphasis. She hoped that he would not be so hooked on fishing, for instance, that other things would be neglected.

It was interesting, indeed, about the second week that Jeff came to the meetings something was said about something that was seen on TV. "Since I don't watch TV I haven't paid that much attention to that?" What? Marie looked out of the corner of her eye to see Cassie's expression. In our day and age to find someone who doesn't watch TV is unusual. She couldn't help but note that that was one of Cassie's things on her list. When she got home she had to mention that to Keith. He raised his eyebrows with interest.

When Cassie's birthday came she planned a special birthday party. She invited a whole host of her friends from the life-style center that she had worked with or become acquainted with. The pastor and his wife from Keith and Marie's church who had given letters of support to her received a special invitation. They had let it be known that she would not be alone, that the church family endorsed her and that she wouldn't be just a subject of the federal system to care for.

The members of the weekly study group came to the party. Her new landlord and wife came, as well as many other friends. It was a special celebration time to Cassie, a time of thankfulness and praise to God for this wonderful opportunity to escape the bloodbath in her own country and to be able to live in a land of freedom.

They each brought a contribution to a scrumptious meal. She'd planned it for "Haystacks" which they all loved: a base of corn chips, piled with beans, tomatoes, lettuce, olives, onions, and a special cheese she'd made from cashews.

Her birthday cake was a most unusual cheesecake—it was made by a French chef. But the unusual thing was that it was made from Tofu. Tofu? Ugh! Who would think of making a cake from Tofu? At first that didn't sound appetizing at all. But what a surprise—it was absolutely delicious!

After the great meal they all took their seats in the open living room and dining area. The little apartment was packed with smiling faces. Cassie gave each a little piece of folded paper. They would each open this piece of paper upon which was written a special Bible promise. They would read their promise and make a comment if they wished about something in their lives for which they were especially thankful.

Then Cassie gave a testimony of how special this birthday was to her and about God's blessings in so many ways to her all through her life and especially to bring her to a new home in a new land where she could really feel God's care in bringing her from a "nobody" to making her the daughter of the King.

She told them of the day she went by the market and found this ad for this apartment for rent. When she called the landlord he said he'd meet her at the market and she could ride with him to see the apartment if she wished. While she was waiting for him to come she had decided, "If he looks strange, I'll drive my own car."

Now at this party, she had a twinkle in her eyes as she quickly said, "I decided to follow in my car!" They all laughed heartily. Even the landlord and his wife laughed. One of the great things about Cassie was her sense of humor! She got that from Grandpa Ivan! Would they ever get to see Grandpa Ivan—the sunshine of her life!

Some of her friends were professional singers. They sang solos, and beautiful harmony in duets and other groups.

Cassie introduced each friend. There was one fellow that she introduced with what seemed to be a special glow. They wondered if there was something there, but as the party went on she didn't pay any more attention to him than any of the rest of them.

Jeff was there as well as several other girls from Bosnia. Jeff visited with these other girls as well.

When the last party guest had gone to their own homes—it was a birthday party they would never forget. As for Keith and Marie, they couldn't help but be a little choked up. Cassie had come to be "their girl"! They loved her so much and were so proud of her in her selection of friends and in her way of celebrating her birthday!

As Cassie had looked for a used sofa she was surprised when a lady at work said she could have a sofa that was just sitting in an empty room. The sofa had a wooden frame with three square cushions of faded chartreuse fabric. Cassie took the sofa home, scrubbed it down from all spider webs, etc., then found a lovely floral throw to cover it with. This was not only her sofa, it was her bed.

As Keith and Marie slept on their comfortable bed at home they couldn't bear to think of Cassie just trying to sleep on that sofa with its three cushions. They were determined just as soon as they could, that they would purchase a bed for her. That time came at the time of her birthday. They had a little truck problem that delayed them reaching her home any sooner and it was a bit late when they arrived

Cassie seemed very happy to finally have a bed and expressed her thanks for this gift. When they started to assemble the frame and set up the bed Cassie expressed the lateness of the hour and said it would be fine to leave the mattresses on the floor, that she could sleep on them as they were for the time being. They knew it would take only about fifteen minutes to assemble it but it was Cassie's home and they would respect her wishes.

They invited Cassie out for their birthday dinner for her. When they came to her home, they were surprised to find that she had asked Jeff if he would come help her set up the bed. She hadn't said anything about him coming. They had showed no special interest in each other. Still this was interesting to them that she would ask Jeff to do this for her when they had every intention to do this. Maybe she just wanted to feel independent. After all she had virtually lived by herself since she was about thirteen and apparently wanted to make her own plans. Who were they to step in the way. They let it go at that.

At the next study group meeting there was no special spark between Cassie and Jeff. He sat over on the sofa; she sat in the chair facing the group. Jeff told the group that he would be graduating from a local college and invited any of them in the group to come to his graduation. Marie thought it would be nice to celebrate this special occasion with him. Cassie called a bit later and asked Marie if she would like to go with her to see him graduate. She was proud of him for going ahead and going to college.

Marie and Cassie were both swallowed up in the crowd of well-wishers of family and friends that night. Cassie spotted him first, "Doesn't Jeff look nice!" she smiled brightly. There he was going down the aisle, his blue silk gown furling at his eager stride. They could see his mom and dad and another worker from where Jeff worked who looked much like a twin to Jeff—they were special friends.

Relatives and friends were whooping, hollering, and whistling as their special candidate received his or her diploma. Jeff's friends applauded loudly for Jeff. Afterwards as Cassie and Marie met with Jeff and his parents they asked them to come to a special light supper at their home to help celebrate. As Cassie and Marie went to the car Marie asked her if she would like to go with Jeff in his car. She said she would feel much better if they went together since she hadn't really met Jeff's parents yet and really didn't even know Jeff that well.

They made arrangements with Jeff to meet him at a certain point where he could lead the way to his parents' home since they'd never been there before. When they met Marie asked Jeff if he would like to go in her car. He said it would be nice since his truck was having some problems at the time. She let Jeff drive her car while she slipped in the back. They had a nice visit as they chatted on the way through the dark.

Jeff's grandmother and aunt and uncle were also there. His mother had made a delicious meal with fruits and cake, chips and dip. They sat around the table and enjoyed the friendship. Since the hour was late and they had to go to work the next morning they soon gave Jeff their well-wishes and made their way home.

On the way home Cassie asked some small question about Jeff's late wife. He remarked about how "easy-going" she had been. Cassie was silent. Marie could almost read her mind, especially since not long before this she had mentioned that maybe she was to be single—maybe she was "too aggressive." Yep, Marie was right, after they'd said good-bye to Jeff and he got in his truck Cassie said, "I don't know. I think he still misses his wife, did you hear him say she was "so easy-going?"

Marie chimed in, "Of course you do miss a husband or wife who has died but you often think of them in a positive way. You tend to remember all the good in them. But when they were alive there was also the good and the bad in each day. You were two individuals, with two different opinions. You didn't always see eye-to-eye. It wasn't always "easy-going" but you learned to give and to take. You learned to be tolerable and respect each other as individuals. The older I grow the more tolerant I am of other people's opinions and choices. Not everyone has to agree with me. I can respect their views even though their views may not be my views. Two people can determine to disagree agreeably."

It was about that time that during the week, at work, Jeff had said he had called Cassie to see if she would like to go out for dinner. She had said to call her a certain time a bit later and she could give him a better answer after she knew more about her schedule. Marie didn't say anything to Cassie about him telling her this. If she wanted to tell Marie she thought she would in her own time. Jeff was really wondering if she did ever like to go out to eat. "Oh, I think she would like to," Marie replied. "I don't see any reason she would turn down an invitation like this."

When he called her again he said she had agreed. Marie still didn't say anything to Cassie. When she wanted to tell her she would. But she was eager to know her thoughts.

It wasn't long until she accepted another invitation and then another. The boss at work saw Jeff come into the Soup and Salad restaurant one day with two motorcycle helmets and of course he had to chide Jeff. They thought they were secretly meeting and hadn't told any one where they were eating out.

Privacy! Privacy! What happened to privacy! Privacy? Who had privacy around a busy community and it's nearby eating arena! Besides didn't everybody know everything about everybody around here!

Jeff had a motorcycle. Cassie hadn't ridden on a motorcycle before. In her country she liked to wear long dresses. It was now the style in the U.S.A. and she still liked the long dresses. How was she to ride a motorcycle in a long dress? Off came the long dresses when she bought some jeans for certain occasions. Cassie held onto Jeff tightly riding in back of him to the restaurants they enjoyed. It was sometimes scary riding in back of Jeff when she was not able to be in control of the driving but Jeff tried to be especially cautious and slow when Cassie was riding with him. After all she'd been through it was no time to have an accident. But once when Cassie was driving the car in back of Jeff who was on the motorcycle she gasped as she saw another car almost hit Jeff. She didn't ride on back of the motorcycle for very long.

When Keith and Marie invited Jeff and Cassie out to dinner on Keith's birthday Cassie was sitting in one corner of the back seat and Jeff was sitting in the other corner. That's odd—who's kidding who—were they holding hands in the middle?

Not long afterward when they came to the weekly study meeting, Jeff wasn't sitting on the sofa; he was sitting in a chair beside Cassie. This time Cassie had asked Jeff if he would be the leader for that night's discussion.

After the next group meeting Jeff and Cassie were sitting next to each other, their fingertips touching as they smiled into each other's eyes.

Then after the next meeting they were holding hands. Something was happening! This was new!

Besides Jeff's full time work he also had a business of his own doing carpentry work. He was an excellent carpenter. Among other items he made some nice pieces of furniture. Jeff's stepfather, now retired was the salesman for the business. They were really doing well as father and son. But it wouldn't be long before Jeff's father was diagnosed with terminal cancer. He had battled cancer for years with recessions but now cancer had spread and suddenly it had grown seriously. Soon he had to give up having a part in the business.

Cassie would go along to help get things set up for the business down at the Convention Center for a trade show. "I'm even climbing up high for some of the displays!" she laughed in disbelief. She couldn't believe that she was actually doing such "crazy" things! Once again she was out of her long skirts and into her jeans not exactly comfortable wearing them but getting used to them.

Jeff and Cassie took some short trips to local attractions, usually nature parks. Once they visited a beautiful park. Standing behind wooden fence barriers they could overlook an awesome valley surrounded by steep hillsides.

Down in the bottom of the valley a cool creek splashed over rocks and ran down the center of the canyon. Several beautiful singing waterfalls fed the creek. It was a day full of splendor. The sun shone brightly. Big, fluffy, white clouds piled high in a mountain of cotton against the brilliant blue of the sky.

The beauty was truly awe-inspiring. Standing overlooking this panorama, holding hands tightly, it struck them both. "Let's have a special prayer of thanks for the beauty of this day that God has provided!" Jeff spoke and Cassie felt even closer to Jeff.

They wandered down the trails of the steep mountain side, stopping to look at each special little flower and on down to the cool waters of the creek and under the spraying waters of the waterfall echoing from the rock walls. Cassie slipped out of her shoes and stuck her feet into the cool waters. It didn't take long for Jeff to do the same. It was truly refreshing. Some of their favorite spots were the ones out in nature, away from the hustle and bustle of a busy world—just "chilling out."

Cassie felt it was really providential when she was offered a job on the grounds of the life-style center but not with the center itself, to sit with an elderly, bed-ridden lady at nights. She grew to really love this lovely lady and they often had chances to talk of Heavenly things and life in general. It was truly inspiring for each of them to hear the experiences of each other. They shared a good friendship these two young and old. But one night in particular the whole household was afraid the elderly lady was slipping off away from them into a coma or even death. They were all afraid for her. Cassie's thoughts were going far away to her own grandmother whom she had learned to appreciate more and more as the days and years went by. After traveling the half hour or so back to her home the next morning after this weary, frightening night Cassie went right to the phone to call her grandparents to tell them how much she loved them and how much they meant to her! Marie was touched to once again experience the true caring of Cassie.

After driving so far through mostly heavy traffic to get back and forth from work it was truly refreshing for Cassie and Jeff to find rest from the stress of their weekly work by visiting a nice, quiet, natural setting.

When Cassie was back from her regular nursing work it seemed she was always working. She cleaned and she baked, she cleaned and she cooked. When would she ever settle down to rest!

Chapter 16

A SPECIAL VALENTINE FOR CASSIE

One day shortly after Valentine's Day when Cassie was home the phone rang. Quickly she picked up the receiver. She and Jeff spent quite a bit of time calling each other these days it seemed. The ringing of the phone was a good sound.

"Can you come for a picnic dinner with me today?" It was Jeff; in fact, it was his birthday! Cassie had planned something special for him for the evening meal but it was such a beautiful day and Jeff sounded so excited that it was very easy to say, "Why, of course, I would love to go to a picnic with you! What do you have in mind? What can I bring?"

"Oh, I've got it all planned. Just leave it with me. When can you come?"

"Just come pick me up anytime you want to!" Cassie giggled.

"How about I come pick you up and we go to that first little picnic table on the Biology Trail?"

"To the Biology Trail it is—great idea!"

"I'll meet you in about an hour—how will that be?"

"The sooner the better," Cassie chirped.

Cassie eagerly waited for Jeff's truck to show up. She had her jacket ready to slip into. It was a sunny day but a bit nippy in February. As soon as Jeff came to her door she was out the door in no time flat. They gave each other a little hug and Jeff held the truck's door open for her.

They chatted merrily the few minutes it took to get to the trail.

As Jeff opened the door for Cassie he reached in the back of the truck for the picnic basket he had neatly packed.

"What do we have for dinner in that picnic basket?" Cassie teased.

"Just wait and see. I hope you'll like it."

"Like it? I'm starving and I know you like the things I like so I can hardly wait to see what it is."

They walked hand-in-hand, arms swinging, feet slipping on the slippery pine needle path until they reached the picnic table.

The old wooden table was falling apart and growing moss but they found the most sturdy part for which to sit across from each other.

The sweet fragrance of the pine needles as the branches were waving in the breeze and their merry little singing sound set for the perfect dinner smells and sweetest dinner music.

"Ta-da-da!" Jeff trilled as he spread the tablecloth on the table.

"Why, Jeff, you even brought a tablecloth! What a thoughtful guy you are!" Cassie was impressed.

"A thoughtful guy," that was music to his ears. He'd never thought of himself as a "thoughtful guy." It had seemed life had become sort of hum-drum until lately when this little lady had come into his life. He loved the way she wrinkled that cute little nose into the cutest little expression as she laughed. He loved to hear her sweet little brogue as she "vondered" (wondered) about certain things and as she asked him about the "vemin" (women) in his life. As for Keith and Marie they hoped she would never give up her cute little accent especially the "but I just vonder" and the "vemin" did this and did that. They knew the longer she lived in America these little things would wear away. But they would always be a part of their memory of Cassie's life.

Jeff brought out the real aroma for this picnic meal with the Subway sandwiches he unwrapped and as he set out the bowls of tomato basil soup from Blimpies they both enjoyed so much. But this day out in the woods, this picnic seemed so very special. It was indeed very special because Jeff had thought of it and down to the last detail.

"Jeff is really good at surprises!" Cassie thought. "What a beautiful picnic surprise!" she excitedly spoke out loud!

Jeff had come to mean more and more to Cassie. She saw that, even though he might seem a more quiet man to some, he wasn't afraid to make his point. She felt secure with Jeff. When she spoke in an aggressive way (a part of her determined personality that she knew she had) Jeff could often quietly turn a situation into one that they could talk about from all sides.

"He's really such a nice guy." Cassie was thinking, "He's not like some guys who are all over you." She really appreciated his morality and thought he had many good traits. "He's an 'easy-going' type for the most part," she thought.

Now they sat side-by-side listening to the sweet sounds of the forest, the trills of the birds, the squeaks of a chipmunk now and then. They watched a spider weaving it's web. "Who taught that spider to make such a neat home—each strand of its silk just so far from the next strand as it weaves its orb!" What a God who cares about even the smallest of His creatures and teaches them the best ways to live their lives.

They were enjoying the quiet sounds of the unhurried wood creatures and wanted to linger even longer in this bliss but time was going by and they each had much to do before the daylight hours ended.

As with one accord they each came back to life and knew it was time to go once more. It was back to the business of the day! But it was Cassie who made the first move. Cassie was ever mindful of time slipping by—something she would perhaps eventually learn in time that if you didn't take time out you would never have time out. It was a way of life for her. This little girl who was called a "nobody" was now stretching her wings. All the things she had wanted to accomplish all her life could now become a reality and someway she felt that already in her thirties time wasn't going to slow down. What she'd always wanted to do she had to pack into this day! She couldn't let a day slip by without feeling accomplishment. It would take a special fellow to understand this constant drive she had within herself! A day in the life of an ordinary American who had had many opportunities would not be the same as the day in the life of someone just being set free who still had so much for which to look forward to.

Cassie yearned to learn, learn, learn. She was a sponge, absorbing everything she studied—wanting to find out more and more. True, she had received her RN in Austria but she felt that in America she needed to learn even more. She would start all over to get her RN degree in America. In so doing, she would have everything down pat in her mind. and she wouldn't stop with getting her RN degree. She would continue to get her master's degree—that would be her goal. She would work and study and never give up. She would need a strong husband to realize these special traits in her. In the end he would be truly blessed to have a wife with these traits but for now some of the times she felt in such a hurry to accomplish things could easily become a hardship to a husband who didn't fully understand.

And it would take a special wife to understand some of Jeff's emotions. At this time he was experiencing reconciliation, forgiveness, and love toward some things in his earlier life. Jeff's life bore mental scars that would still take time to heal. It would take a wife who understood these wounds to fully help Jeff with his future.

Even though it was Cassie who made the first move to be on their way before the daylight hours ended the other work they had to do for this day Jeff, too, knew that they must be on their way, "but slow down just a little," he wanted to say. "I haven't said all I want to say."

They neatly folded the tablecloth and placed it back in the picnic basket.

"That was such a delicious picnic." You were so thoughtful, Jeff! I thoroughly enjoyed this time together!"

They slowly strolled back down the trail, savoring each moment together.

Jeff walked along more thoughtful than ever—finally he just couldn't wait any longer. He sat the picnic basket down on the ground.

Cassie stopped, wondering what was the matter.

Grasping each of Cassie's hands in his he pulled her around to face him. "Cassie, you mean the world to me. I love your very much. Will you marry me?"

Although he'd been rehearsing these words for some time it was now so easy to say because the words came from his heart.

This was a real surprise for Cassie and her heart did a little skip. But it didn't take her long to respond, "Oh, Jeff—I love you too. Yes, I accept!" And all of a sudden they were holding each other in a warm and tight embrace. As they gave each other a special kiss of commitment they could feel each other's heart beating wildly. So what if someone else might be coming down the trail. It didn't matter. This moment was their's—the whole rest of the world was shut out. This was now their little world of love. It was hard to leave this peaceful forest which was now their special place in memory of the love they shared as they committed themselves to each other. Jeff had finally caught Cassie! Jeff captured Cassie's heart. Love was abloom in February as much as it was in the springtime!

They were both ecstatic as they started thinking more and more of a home together and of their wedding day! Talk about stars! There were twinkling stars in their eyes that could not be hidden.

Cassie had always looked forward to her wedding day like most young girls. She had helped many of her friends with their weddings. In her country the weddings took a great deal of planning down to the last detail. They were usually BIG weddings. So now the wheels started turning as she dreamed of her wedding.

Not long afterwards Jeff and Cassie invited Keith and Marie for a picnic at a lovely park along with Jeff's mom and some of their close friends. They munched on chips, potato salad, sandwiches, sliced tomatoes, dessert and drinks. And then when things quieted down a bit Jeff said they had something to tell them. His eyes were bright, Cassie was beaming. "We're getting married!" They all bubbled over with congratulations as they looked first at one and then the other of the happy couple with big smiles. They were so happy for them!

"When's the date?" they all asked at once.

"We're getting married July the 16th," they excitedly answered.

As the days went by the doctors gave bad news that Jeff's father only had a very short time to live. Keith and Marie visited him in the hospital and listened to his words of cheer and they hoped some miracle would happen, but in their hearts they knew that if a miracle didn't happen, he was growing weaker and weaker. He was in a great deal of pain. He was so very happy for Jeff and Cassie.

Jeff and Cassie felt that Dad just might not be with them by July 16. Many thoughts of preparation went through Cassie's head for the wedding.

One day in April Jeff and Cassie stopped by Keith and Marie's home for a visit. Their eyes were bright—they held a secret.

"We got married down at the Court House," they excitedly told them. "There was so much stress at this time with Jeff's dad being so ill and wondering if he would even make it until July 16, plus stress with work—we felt it was just too much to plan a big wedding. We got married out on the lawn of the Court House."

They were surprised! They were already married! But they understood the reason for not waiting and tears were in their eyes as they wished them the best for life. She was "their" girl! They loved her dearly. They wanted the very best for the happy couple.

Jeff and Cassie stopped by their house on their way to their honeymoon to the Smokies. Cassie was in shorts—she had legs after all. They'd never seen her legs, they were always under a long skirt or in jeans. Truly she was becoming a Westerner! They had a beautiful time in a little cabin once again away from the flurry of the busy world of work and travel back and forth to work for Cassie.

Now, they, too, didn't have the financial burden of a big wedding.

As time slowed down they wanted to have their wedding vows said in front of a minister at church. They planned their own reception and Marie added a note to the invitation that this would also be a wedding shower for them.

The evening was beautiful. Friends came from many miles away to wish them the very best. It was so special to hear them pledge their lives together. This little girl from far away across the wide ocean called a "Nobody" was now in the Land of the Free with no fears—with a home and bright future for which to look forward. "I don't wish for a big house with a swimming pool" (they'd heard her say to the news media on TV). "I just wish for freedom—a place to live where my children can grow up safely."

Before this event could take place Jeff's father passed away. It was a sad time for family and friends but after all the pain that he had gone through for many years, they knew that he needed this relief. They felt that his spiritual life showed that he truly had given himself to his Master. Now they could look forward to the Great Resurrection Day when once again they would see him—only this time all pain would be gone forever.

Chapter 17

CASSIE INDUCTED INTO ALPHA BETA MU CHAPTER

A special Honor. Cassie invited Keith and Marie to her induction to the Alpha Beta Mu chapter. Today, a beautiful, sunny day in March as they drove the few miles to the site of this special ceremony, tears filled Marie's eyes and sobs choked her voice.

"I've got to stop these tears before I see Cassie," she jabbered, her chin quivering and her chest heaving. "Just think, she almost didn't make it. She could so easily have lost her life!" Memories of not so long ago when they fought for her life and waited so many days for the answer to her asylum welled up within her.

"No one else really knows what an accomplishment this is today for Cassie!"

You could see the flood of memories tugging at Keith's heart, too. They shared a secret world within themselves—a heartache so near—they could have lost her so easily.

But once again the tears broke away to sunshine as they saw her march down the aisle, and they were so proud of her as she stood with the rest of the "cream of the crop." Their eyes were glued to the screen, their ears attune to Stacey Allison, the brave woman who made it to the top of Mt. Everest, addressing a similar group.

She did not make it to the top on her first quest. There was disappointment—there were valleys of despair—but there's a difference between failure and giving up, she emphasized.

Failure is only temporary. Giving up is permanent. For Stacey, the thought of taking the chance of dying while determined to reach the top of Mt. Everest was completely alien. For Cassie, one chance of life seemed to have more important goals. Still, the thoughts of success Stacey was relating made a big impact.

When Stacey's group disembarked from the plane they wanted to rush into customs, grab their gear, and be on their way. It was disappointing to be told to come "tomorrow"—to stop and have some tea. Tea? That was the last thing on their minds. But wait they must and after waiting several more days before being given their gear they learned a life-long lesson—that while on the way upward to success one must stop to understand family and friends—to listen carefully to the important things of **their** lives—not just to do what **you** wanted so urgently to do.

Once Stacey could see a much faster way to get from point A to point B and she rushed for the shortcut. What she didn't know was in her rush through the shortcut, leeches were falling from the foliage onto her and attaching in her armpits, her groin, onto her legs. When she ran back to the rest of her group, with blood streaks all over her body, she was crying, "Help me! Help me!" She was very grateful for their help in getting rid of the bloodsuckers. Short cuts were not always the best plan, she determined.

At another time one of the leaders thought it best to forget plan A and to go to his plan B but the others were so bent on plan A so he went along with the group. A great roar was heard as a great wall of snow engulfed them.

The avalanche caught eight of their group. When the roar had ended and the tons of snow had thundered down the valleys rushing over everything in its path and heavily covering everything that struggled—it was so fortunate that all eight were alive and safe. The leader was their hero for listening to their desires and taking a chance to go along with the group.

Success—for some it means striving to be at the very top. for Cassie it seemed it was the only way to go—no in between. She'd prayed to be "Somebody" not just an ordinary person in a little far away place.

For Cassie "God Makes Everything Beautiful in **His** Time!"

It was truly an honor to become a member of the Alpha Beta Mu chapter. It will be the height of accomplishment when The Ruler of the Universe declares: "You have been faithful in the little things, I will make you ruler of much!" **That** will be the greatest of all accomplishments. Then she will **truly** become "Somebody." But for now Cassie can rejoice in the thought that being "Somebody" here on Earth means being The Child of The King! Her Father is the only one that truly saved her—saved her life for eternity—and saved her life "in the land of the living here on Earth!"

Chapter 18
AN EXTRA SPECIAL VISITOR

Jeff and Cassie had the opportunity to rent a little cottage out in the country from a man Jeff worked with. It was out on some country acreage where they could hear the Canada geese down by the stream and the spring frogs peeping. They could have their own garden; they both enjoyed gardening. It was quiet and tranquil.

Once again they started having a few friends over once a week to spend an hour or two studying the Bible together, sharing words of encouragement and inspiration. As they sipped fresh hot cider and nibbled on a few cookies it was a special time to keep in touch with friends they could only see in passing during the busy week.

Cassie determined to complete her RN degree in the States even though she had already received this degree in Austria. With a new language, different medications, different medical procedures she wanted to give her patients the very best treatment. It was not easy juggling work with studies and have a great home life.

What a privilege it had been for Cassie to be able to take care of the elderly bed-ridden patient for so many months. She really enjoyed the little lady and they shared so many moments of inspiration together. It was like sitting at the feet of a special counselor for Cassie. The elderly lady had so many years of wonderful experiences but now she too needed the care of the cheerful Cassie to get her through the hard times of growing older.

But the sad day came when this lady's estate finally ran out of being able to afford a private nurse. Now work must be doubled up with some of the other help and it was time for Cassie to move on to other work. As the little lady had said to Cassie on many occasions, "God will take care of it all!" She found work at a hospital closer to home while doing her nursing studies. Happily she found her supervisors to be quite understanding of her work and study schedule.

Cassie learned Grandpa had been shedding tears saying he was afraid he'd never get to see his Cassie again. So Jeff and Cassie saved up and bought Grandpa a ticket to come to America for a few weeks!

It was one big happy day when they met Grandpa at the airport a couple of hours away from home. When Grandpa came down the ramp to the airport his big smile and glistening eyes reflected the same big smile from Cassie! It was a wonderful day to see her "Sunshine" once again.

Grandpa felt an obligation to do something to help—it was just a part of his nature, so he worked hard out in the garden pulling weeds and keeping house. Jeff and Cassie were gone so much with work and studies but at least Grandpa got to see that his Cassie was well and safe. Since Grandpa knew very little English and had no driver's license, etc., he had to wait for Jeff and Cassie to take him anywhere.

Many months before Keith and Marie had been part of a group who had helped Bosnian refugees to get settled in their new home in America. They seemed like family to them. Keith decided it would be fun to take these kids as translators and take them and Grandpa to the lake for a swim on a hot day.

The lake had beach sand brought in for the swimming area. Grandpa eagerly took off his shoes and walked in the sand with the kids. He had a big smile on his face as he shuffled his feet through the sand. They all seemed to be having a great time. But Grandpa kept worrying about the cost of gas. It seems that was a big factor in their country. When Keith offered to take them other places during Grandpa's stay here, that cost of gas still bothered him greatly and he couldn't seem to relax thinking Keith was spending too much.

Grandpa gave Keith and Marie a special treat by inviting them over for a meal he had prepared It was absolutely delicious and they cherished this time with him—this grand man whom they'd heard so much about and longed to meet. He'd seemed so real before they'd even seen him but now his short stature stood tall before their eyes. His sparkling personality exuded extra special love and care not only for his beloved granddaughter but they could see him bending over that young boy who lay dying in front of his house. They could feel his heart of tenderness toward this innocent, undeserving boy and his righteous anger toward those who took his life.

They could see him sorrowfully step by step making his way to his own door only to hear the shout that he must leave. But he could only endure the heartache for days and years to follow. But he knew there is a God and that God makes all things beautiful in His time.

All too soon it was time for Grandpa to get back on the silver wings that would carry him back home to tell Grandma that Cassie was well and safe.

Cassie had said that a big house was not her primary dream. Her grandest hope was for freedom and to be treated as a human regardless of name, of religion, of gender, of ethnic ways. But it was so great that she and Jeff now were able to purchase their own home, and a "Big" home at that! Now they were able to plan for better days in the future.

It was cute, Jeff had spoken of wanting a dog. Cassie shied away from dogs. She'd never grown up with pets.

But one day after they got their new home Keith and Marie were invited over to see their new puppy. They were both highly surprised. But Cassie loved that little, white, soft puppy. She'd taught him some tricks—the bond was struck. Not long afterward they got another puppy to be a playmate for the first puppy. She has pictures of her "kids" at her work station.

Some months before, Jeff had a motorcycle accident and had broken a leg which had to be pinned. It was a long, painful, slow recovery. Since their insurance didn't cover motorcycle accidents they were on their own; this seemed to be the straw that broke the camel's back. It was tough, no getting around it.

But in spite of this lesson in the school of hard knocks something really good came of it. This trial was turned into a blessing after all. Jeff's work involved him doing a lot of carpentry work but his knees were giving out. Now, since the accident happened, he could not do some types of carpentry work but he'd been taking computer classes—the right kind of computer lessons that would fit right into work needs at the shop where he worked.

The dark epic of the broken leg turned into the sunlight of a new career. Once again God makes all things beautiful in His time.

Keith went to the doctor one day feeling extremely weak and having a great deal of pain. After a few inches of the EKG ribbon, the nurse stopped the EKG, called an ambulance and sent him to the hospital. He was going into a heart attack. At the hospital his oxygen arterial level was found to be dangerously low, only 40 instead of the 100 it should have been. His weakness was from organs not getting enough oxygen—they were dying.

When Cassie broke away from her busy schedule to visit Keith at the hospital her cheerful presence gave them all a jump start.

It seems Cassie will always be their "miracle girl." It's a miracle she didn't have to go through the blood bath in Yugoslavia with her own countrymen. It's a miracle Keith and Marie were able to meet her at the time that they did and under the circumstances that they did. It's a miracle she's in the Land of the Free. It's possible she could think, "if it hadn't have been Keith and Marie someone would be able to help, it could have happened some other way," and that is positively true. But it didn't happen that way and they're so ever thankful to have been a part in God's plan for Cassie's continued life. They cherish this experience. They love watching Cassie's future grow. She will always be so special to them.

Yes, Marie proudly watched Cassie march down the graduation line as she received her RN degree here in America, another dream come true. Although she's busy with her hospital patients, making them feel comfortable, giving away her cheerful smile—she's at it again. You guessed it, she's still taking classes, still climbing the ladder. Expect to see more degrees, more graduations. Where there's a will there's a way. Her spirit of learning, learning will continue to bring her success and make the world a better place in which to live. Long live Cassie, the butterfly that knows the spirit of freedom that many of us in America take for granted. She's really SOMEBODY!

* * * * *

The following pages are some very special articles that Cassie wrote.

She spent many hours trying and testing every single recipe and was truly fascinated in learning a new way to cook, healthfully.

The author received permission to publish these as a special surprise to Cassie to conclude this book. The editor of the magazine is a very special jewel who has been a wonderful friend of the author as they worked together several years in the production of the magazine. Cassie counts it a real privilege to have this dear lady as both a friend and mentor.

So long for now from
Jeff and Cassie,
Keith and Marie.

Have fun; stay healthy, live a long, cheerful life; be kind to your neighbors. "Do unto others as you would have them do unto you!"

Don't forget the way the Lord has kept you in the past and be assured He will not permit anything to come to you that He knows you cannot bear. He will be beside you giving you His strength all the way!

Be sure to reserve your home in the New Earth. We plan to be there! See you there!

• • •

Late Breaking News!!! It's a girl! Jeff and Cassie are blessed with a little miracle, a baby girl!

COME, LET'S EAT JEWISH

What is Jewish cooking? Ask people whose parents or ancestors came from Russia, France, Poland, Austria, Germany, Czechoslovakia, Hungary, Spain, England, Persia, and Israel, and you will hear completely different answers. For me, Jewish cooking is linked inextricably with memories of a two-week vacation in Israel, and trying many Jewish dishes while living in New York. I can still smell Israeli falafels and halvah sold in the small stores of Old Jerusalem; humus and pita bread in a tiny restaurant close to Jericho; crepes, latke, and cakes in a buffet of a hotel at the Red Sea. Of course, challah is something special to find everywhere.

Painful experience it is if you only smell but do not eat. Most of those dishes are loaded with fats, dairy, eggs, and meat. Conscientious about my health, I could not enjoy them very much and hoped that one day I would be able to prepare them in a healthier way. Dreams become reality! So never stop dreaming!!!

Today I am especially excited about the relationship between a certain food and Jewish holidays.

"Remember the Sabbath day, to keep it holy." Exodus 20:8. Shabbat, the Sabbath day, a day set aside for prayer, reflection, and the reinforcement of family ties, has been a source of strength for Jews throughout the centuries. Challah is the traditional Jewish braided bread which is served at weekly Shabbat meals.

Our recipe uses all whole wheat flour and dispenses with eggs in order to create a delicious but more healthful Sabbath and holiday treat.

Stuffed cabbage and humus are traditional foods that are served on Sykkoth (the Jewish Thanksgiving), a Hebrew word meaning booths, huts or tents, which celebrates the fall harvest and commemorates the Hebrews' years of wandering in the desert after the Exodus from Egypt.

The Talmud considers Shavuot as the day that Moses received the Ten Commandments on Mt. Sinai. It is customary to serve dishes like blintzes. No article on Jewish cooking would be complete without a recipe for blintzes. You might call them crepes, palacsinken or blini and fill them with apricot jam or blueberry, but they are still blintzes. They may be made ahead of time and kept in the refrigerator for two to three days or frozen for future use. You can also freeze them filled.

For children, the happiest and most memorable holiday of the Jewish calendar is Hanukkah with its eight days of lighting candles, singing songs, opening presents, playing games, having fun, and eating traditional potato pancakes (in Yiddish, the word for pancake is *latke*).

Halvah is a delicious dessert eaten typically during Purim, a spring holiday that commemorates Esther, the favorite Jewish queen of Persia, and her rescue of the Jews from the evil Haman. This holy day shows that good is triumphant over evil, and a person has a right to be different, even if he or she is in the minority.

Independence Day, celebrated each year in mid-May, is the anniversary of the creation, in 1948, of the new state of Israel. On this special day for the Israeli nation, traditional Israeli falafel are eaten.

The incidence of heart disease, diabetes, high blood pressure, and colon cancer in the Jewish population—orthodox, nonobservant, and in between—is inordinately high. There is no conclusive evidence to determine whether the critical factor is genetic or cultural, but since we can't manipulate our genes, we owe it to ourselves to eat healthfully. Recognize that a low-fat, no-cholesterol, high-fiber diet will not only lengthen your life, but also improve its quality. Make this style of eating the habit of a lifetime. *L'chaim!*

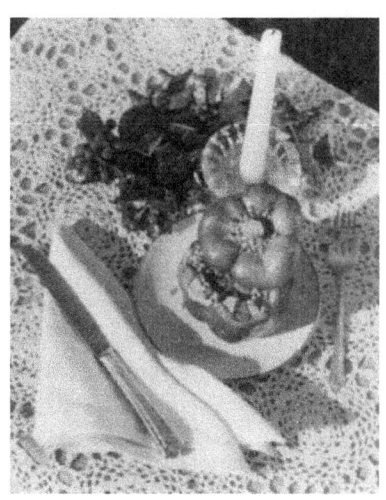

STUFFED PEPPERS

4–6	green bell peppers
1½ cup	cooked whole-grain rice
1 large	onion, chopped and sauteed in water
2 stalks	celery, chopped and sauteed in water
1 cup	sliced carrots, sauteed in water
1 cup	green ripe olives, sliced
2 cloves	garlic, minced
2 cups	tomato sauce (spice free), #1
2 Tbs.	yeast flakes
½ cup	sunflower seeds
2 Tbs.	parsley
1 tsp.	paprika, mild
1 cup	tomato sauce (spice free), #2

Mix all ingredients and stuff the peppers. Pour 1 cup tomato sauce (#2) into an ungreased baking dish. Place stuffed bell peppers in the dish. Bake in oven at 350 for 45 minutes.

ISRAELI FALAFEL BALLS

2 cups	cooked garbanzo beans
1 large	onion, chopped
2 Tbs.	parsley, chopped
¾ tsp.	salt
4 cloves	garlic, minced
¼ tsp.	cumin
¼ tsp.	coriander
½ cup	bulgur wheat, soaked
¼ cup	soy flour

Combine all ingredients except bulgur wheat in a food processor. Add bulgur wheat and mix until the mixture forms a small ball without sticking to your hands. Refrigerate at least one hour. Form into balls. Bake at 350 until brown (about 30 minutes). May be frozen.

TAHINI SAUCE FOR FALAFELS

½ cup	tahini
1 cup	cooked garbanzos
6 Tbs.	lemon juice
1 clove	garlic, minced, or ½ tsp. garlic powder
3 Tbs.	soy sauce
water as needed	

Blend all ingredients, adding water as needed to thicken as desired. Open whole wheat pita halves into pockets and spread the bottom with soy mayonnaise. Fill with chopped lettuce or grated cabbage, and four falafel balls topped with sliced olives, chopped tomatoes, onions, bell pepper, and cucumbers. Drizzle with two or three tablespoons of Tahini Sauce.

PATE (VEGETARIAN "CHOPPED LIVER")

1 cup	cooked lentils
½ cup	pecan or walnut meats
1	10-oz package frozen string beans, cooked
2 large	onions sauteed in water
1 Tbs.	unfermented soy sauce
1 tsp.	chicken-style seasoning
	garlic salt to taste

Grind all ingredients. Add seasonings. Mix well and refrigerate to blend flavors. Spread on *Matzoh* (unleavened bread eaten especially at Passover), garnish with vegetables and parsley, and serve as hors d'oeuvres.

HUMUS (CHICK-PEA PUREE)

2 cups	cooked garbanzos
½ cup	tahini
⅓ cup	lemon juice
1 clove	garlic
1 ⅛ tsp.	salt
2 tsps.	onion powder
⅓–½ cup	water

Blend all together in a blender or food processor, adding water as needed to thicken as desired. Refrigerate at least two hours for flavors to blend. Garnish with parsley and serve as a dip for whole wheat pita bread cut into triangles, and bite-sized, fresh vegetables such as carrots, celery, broccoli, cauliflower, and zucchini.

LATKES (POTATO PANCAKES)

1 tsp.	vitamin C or 1 vitamin C tablet (ascorbic acid prevents browning.)
4	potatoes, shredded
1	onion, shredded
1 tsp.	salt
1	carrot, shredded
2 Tbs.	yeast flakes
2 Tbs.	parsley
2 Tbs.	whole wheat flour

Place vitamin C in a bowl, with two tablespoons hot water to dissolve. Add potatoes, onion, and carrot. Add whole wheat flour, salt, parsley, and yeast flakes and stir until incorporated. Spoon onto a baking sheet and flatten. Bake until golden on both sides. Serve with soy sour cream or mayonnaise.

PALACSINKEN (CREPES)

2 cups	whole wheat flour
2 cups	quick oats
¾ tsp.	salt
4 cups	water or soy milk
2 Tbs.	oil, extra-virgin olive oil preferred
1 Tbs.	vanilla or maple flavoring
2 Tbs.	honey

Blend ingredients or mix together in a bowl, blending two cups at a time until smooth, emptying into another bowl and repeating until all is blended. Pour ½ cup batter onto lightly sprayed or oiled skillet heated on medium-high. Quickly spread with bottom of measuring cup or spoon. When edges are cooked and bottom is brown, flip to brown on other side. Place filling of your choice (tofu cottage cheese, cooked fruit) in center and roll up. When filling with fruit, top with no-dairy whipped cream of your choice.

CHALLAH

⅓ cup	oatmeal
6 cups	whole wheat flour
½ cup	gluten flour
1 Tbs.	instant yeast
1 tsp	salt
⅓ cup	honey
2 cups	warm water
1 cup	applesauce
1 cup	raisins
1 tsp	turmeric in ¼ cup soy milk
	Sesame seeds

Mix first five ingredients and set aside. Mix honey, water and applesauce and add to the dry mixture. Knead briefly to mix thoroughly. Let sit for five minutes. Knead for 10 minutes. Add one cup of raisins and knead them in. Let rise until double in bulk.

Punch down, then place dough on a lightly-floured board and knead until smooth about two minutes. Divide dough into three pieces, then roll each piece with your hands into a long, smooth rope about ¾ inch wide.

Lay pieces side by side on a sprayed baking sheet. Pinch the three pieces together at one end then braid them. Pinch other end, and tuck both ends under.

Let rise at room temperature until double. Brush with soy milk and turmeric mixture and sprinkle with sesame seeds.

Bake for about one hour at 350 degrees or until golden-brown and hollow-sounding when tapped. Remove from baking sheet and cool on wire rack.

(*Preferably wait at least a day before eating fresh baked bread, allowing some unhealthy gaseous products of yeast fermentation to escape. Bread can then be slightly sprinkled and reheated for greater enjoyment. Ed.*)

HALVAH

2 cups	tahini
2 cups	soy milk powder
½ cup	honey
2 Tbs.	vanilla, maple, or peppermint extract
½ cup	walnuts or hazelnuts, chopped

Thoroughly mix all ingredients by hand. Press mixture into an approximately 6" x 8" baking dish. Refrigerate to stiffen. Sprinkle with coconut if desired. Cut into small servings because it is very rich.

LEMON SAUCE (for Apple Cake on next page)

3 cups	pineapple juice
6 ½ Tbs.	cornstarch
½ cup	honey
½ tsp	salt
¼ cup	lemon juice
1 Tbs.	grated lemon rind

Blend all ingredients, except lemon rind, for 20 seconds. Empty into sauce pan, add lemon rind and cook on medium-high, stirring constantly until thick.

APPLE CAKE

2 cups	oat flour
2 cups	whole wheat flour
1 tsp	salt
1 Tbs.	coriander
1 tsp.	anise
1 1/3	cup warm water
2 Tbs.	honey
2 Tbs.	yeast
1 Tbs.	vanilla
2/3 cup	honey, #2
3	chopped apples
1/2 cup	chopped walnuts
1/2 cup	apple sauce

Combine first five (dry) ingredients in a bowl and stir together well. In a small bowl mix together next three ingredients. Set aside for 10-15 minutes to bubble to make a sponge. While sponge is bubbling, mix together next five ingredients in a bowl, and set aside. When sponge is fully bubbled, add liquid ingredients to dry ones. Stir together well. Immediately pour batter into a round, oiled cake pan and spread evenly. Do not let rise, but bake in preheated 375 degree oven for 15 minutes. Reduce temperature to 350 degrees and bake 30 minutes more. When cake is done remove from pan and cool on wire rack. Allow to sit a day before being eaten. To serve, cover top with Lemon Sauce, sprinkle with coconut, and top with a dollop of soy whipped cream

Millet Manna

It was a hot and dry October day in 1996 in the middle of the Sinai Desert, today the territory of Egypt. Along the dusty road Bedouins were selling water, souvenirs, and grains. One grain caught my eye. It was yellow and flaky and looked like small seeds. My thought traveled back 4,000 years; back to the time when the people of Israel had just been freed from slavery in Egypt and were traversing this region—all around them only a vast expanse of nothingness, a stony wilderness. No promise of food, no hidden oasis to give hope of survival. But the God of Israel is indeed omnipotent and gave them "Manna (which) was like small seed, whitish yellow in color..." (Numbers 11:7-9; Exodus 16: 14-21. *The Bible*, TEV). Their needs were abundantly supplied; they lacked for nothing.

Is it perhaps possible that we, too, in this modern age have been given manna from heaven but do not know it? A nutritious, tiny, round yellowish seed is grown in North America, primarily for bird seed and cattle feed. Only a small part of the total crop is processed for human consumption. What is this tiny seed? Can it be that our pets have better food than we do? That our animals are being fed heavenly manna?

This manna is millet. Millet is a grain that has been cultivated in India, Africa, and the Middle East since time immemorial. In Ancient Egypt millet was used to make bread, and it was a staple in China before rice was introduced. Botanically, this grass is more ancient than rice, barley, wheat, or rye. Particularly well suited to poor soil and adverse climates, millet manages to lie dormant through long periods of drought, then sprouts with the first rainfalls and is ready to harvest in just 45 days.

Millet has straight, slender, prominently joined stems (from 3-8 feet, or 0.9-2 meters long and about an inch thick) which terminate in spikes, panicles, or racemes that bear small shiny seeds.

It is the chief source of carbohydrates for about one-third of the world's population, primarily used in India, Africa, and northern China.

The smallest of our familiar grains, millet surpasses whole wheat and brown rice as a rich source of B-complex vitamins and protein. The protein, however, is incomplete, because it does not contain adequate amounts of all amino acids that we must obtain from our food. But it is possible to complete it by eating or combining millet with foods such as legumes, nuts, and other seeds that contain complementary amino acids.

It contains lecithin, an important component of bile, which emulsifies food fats into small droplets and this way speeds up their digestion. This makes the fat more accessible to fat-splitting enzymes. Millet also contains the minerals calcium, iron, magnesium, phosphorus, and potassium. Millet has no gluten, and so cannot be used for raised breads. It is considered to be one of the least allergenic and most easily digestible of all grains, as well as one of the most outstanding alkaline foods in the world.

Millet is rich in fiber which detoxifies the intestines and forms butyric acid, and short-chain fatty acid that has been shown to suppress the growth of cancers; it also contains silica. It is anti-fungal, and is one of the best grains for those with candida problems.

Millet can be cooked in the same way as rice, using three parts water to one part grain. It cooks in 30-45 minutes. You combine a measured amount of grain and liquid, bring the combination to a boil, cover, reduce the heat to very low and cook until the grain absorbs the liquid.

Millet will come out more separate and fluffier if you add it to the pot after the water is already boiling. If the grain is kept fluffy and undisturbed while simmering it will be fluffy and separate. However, if it is stirred frequently and a little liquid is added from time to time, the millet will have a creamy consistency. Lightly toasting millet in a dry pan before cooking enhances its nutty flavor and imparts a lighter fluffier texture to the grain. Place it in a pan and stir constantly over moderate heat for 5-10 minutes until dry and lightly toasted.

Millet is naturally neutral in taste and therefore can be combined with any selection of your favorite flavorings, sweet or savory. For breakfast, prepare it as millet butter, a healthy spread for your bread; or millet waffles with your favorite topping; or as a simple millet hot cereal with some nuts and fruits. Millet loaf or millet patties served with fresh salad, sauteed vegetables and beans would make a delicious lunch. You surely wouldn't want to miss a nutritious dessert like carob pudding or vanilla pie!

Take the time and enjoy God-given manna. The following recipes say, "Try me, I taste as good as I look!" You almost can feel guilty for enjoying them, but they're so good for you. You can scratch the guilt and enjoy yummy food and a clear conscience.

MILLET MANNA

Recipes that look good, taste good, and are good for you!

MILLET LOAF

1. group 1
2   minced garlic cloves

2. group 2
3 Tbs.   extra virgin olive oil
1 cup   uncooked millet
2 cups   chopped onions
1½ cup   chopped celery
1 cup   chopped green pepper
½ cup   shredded carrots

3. group 3
6 cups   canned tomatoes
            (without juice)

4. group 4
1 tsp   basil
1 tsp   salt
2 tsp   onion powder
½ tsp   oregano
½ cup   chopped black olives
½ cup   sunflower seeds.

In pot, saute garlic in enough water to keep from sticking. Add group 2 next three ingredients, and continue to heat for 20 more minutes. Briefly blend canned tomatoes at top speed, and add to millet mixture. Add group 4 ingredients; stir together well. Bring to boil, reduce heat, cover and simmer until liquid is absorbed (about 45 minutes.) Remove from heat. Stir in sunflower seeds. Put into sprayed 8" x 8" baking dish. Bake at 350 degrees for 30 minutes.

MILLET PATTIES

3 cups	cooked millet
2 cups	bread crumbs
1 cup	dry rolled oats
1 tsp	salt
1 tsp	garlic powder
1 medium	chopped onion
1 Tbs.	dried parsley
1 tsp	Spanish paprika
1 tsp	celery seeds
½ cup	fine shredded carrots (optional)
1 cup	cashew pieces and 1 cup water, blended.

Mix together all ingredients except cashews. Add blended cashews and mix well. Form into patties and place on a nonstick cookie sheet. Bake at 350 degrees for 30 minutes. Serve with salad, vegetables, and your favorite gravy, or in sandwiches.

Yield: 9 patties.

MILLET BUTTER

¼ cup   blanched almonds
1 tsp   salt
1 Tbs.   Emes gel, unflavored
1½ cup   water
¼ cup   cooked millet, hot

Stir the Emes gel into the water and heat until the gel is clear. Put the nuts in the blender with the ½ cup water while it is still warm, and blend until the nuts are creamy, then add rest of water. Add the millet and salt, and blend until smooth. Pour the contents into containers. Place into the refrigerator to set.

Yield: 12 1-cup serving bowls.

MILLET BUTTER—alternate recipe

6 cups   water
1 cup   uncooked millet
⅓ cup   tahini
1 Tbs.   salt
1   sweet potato, raw
             coconut to taste (optional)

Bring water to a boil, add all remaining ingredients and simmer for 1 hour. Blend until smooth. Cool and serve. Can be stored in glass jars in refrigerator for about 1 week.

VANILLA-ORANGE PIE

⅓ cup	cashew pieces
½ cup	cooked hot millet
⅓ cup	honey
¼ tsp	salt
1 tsp	vanilla
1 tsp	orange flavoring
4 Tbs.	cornstarch
2 ½ cups	pineapple juice

Place all ingredients in blender with just one cup of the pineapple juice and blend until smooth—at least one minute. Add remaining 1½ cup of pineapple juice at the end. Place in a saucepan and bring to a boil,stirring constantly. Pour immediately into pre-baked pie crust layered with banana slices and chill. A delicious, smooth-as-custard dessert or breakfast treat. Spare the eggs, spare the salmonella…enjoy peace of mind and a pleasurable palate!

PIE CRUST

1 cup	coconut
1 cup	regular oats
¼ tsp	salt
5 Tbs.	water

Blend first two ingredients on high until smooth (15-20 seconds). Pour into bowl and add remaining ingredients. Mix together well with hands. Press evenly into nine-inch pie plate. Bake at 400 degrees for 20 minutes and fill with pie filling. Delicious served with a topping of *Cashew Fruit Cream* or strawberry and banana slices!

CASHEW FRUIT CREAM

1 cup	pineapple juice
¼ tsp	cardamom
⅛ tsp	salt
¼ tsp	anise
½ cup	cashews

Combine all ingredients, blend until smooth, and serve.

MILLET WAFFLES

1 cup	soaked soybeans
3 cups	pineapple juice
10 Tbs.	honey
1½ cups	regular oats
1½ cups	uncooked millet
1 tsp	salt
2 tsp	vanilla flavoring
2 tsp	maple flavoring
2 tsp	pineapple flavoring
1 tsp	coriander
1 tsp	cardamom
¼ cup	coconut

Prepare waffle iron by brushing lightly with oil or spraying with *Pam*. Close lid and preheat on high 5–8 minutes. Blend all ingredients together well. When waffle iron is hot, sprinkle sesame seeds on bottom of iron to reduce chance of waffles sticking and add flavor. Pour batter over seeds and sprinkle more seeds on top of batter. Close lid and bake 10–12 minutes.

Yield: 2 x 9" x 9"

For a very simple yet pleasing alternative waffle recipe, simply add enough hot water to cooked millet to make a thick batter. Spoon onto a waffle iron and cook for at least 10 minutes. The thicker the mixture, the longer the cooking time, and the heavier the waffle. (A good way to use leftover cereal.)

CAROB PUDDING

1 cup	cooked millet
1 package	Mori-Nu soft tofu
2 cups	water
2 Tbs.	Emes gel
½ cup	date pieces
4	soft pitted prunes
⅓ cup	honey
1 tsp.	vanilla
¼ tsp.	salt
2 tsp.	Roma or Pero
¼ tsp.	almond extract
½ cup	carob powder

Place tofu, millet, dates, prunes, and water in a saucepan and bring to a boil. Blend hot millet mixture in blender along with Emes gel for at least two minutes while adding remaining ingredients. Pour hot pudding into containers and refrigerate for several hours until chilled.

Yield: four servings.

ITALIAN CUISINE

AUTHENTICALLY ITALIAN <u>AND</u> HEALTHFUL

The land of vibrant, expressive people has given the world pasta and pizza, Michelangelo and DaVinci, Verdi, and Pavarotti. It is Italy, a country where eating is one of life's great pleasures. What a privilege it was for me to enjoy original and simple Italian cuisine on a vacation through Italy. Today I am so happy to be able to offer egg- and dairy-free Italian dishes. It sounds impossible—pizza without cheeses, tirmisu without eggs???! The good news is—it *is* possible.

Pizza is probably the most famous Italian bread. It is a child of Naples, and nowhere does it taste better. At first, pizzas were flat bread dressed with oil, salt, herbs, and occasionally cheese. Today's favorite fast-food pizzas are quick and filling meals, suitable for all tastes, with toppings that have become far more generous and varied than the traditional Italian pizzas.

For Italians, pasta seems almost as essential to life as water and the love of it is deeply woven into everyday daily life. Of the many types of Italian pasta, spaghetti is perhaps the most loved. The image of spaghetti has come a long way. Once a poor man's staple, spaghetti today is a dish for all occasions. It can be found in elegant restaurants, fast-food shops, and in the homes of Italians regardless of their social status. Remember that pasta does not wait for anyone. It is usually most enjoyed if served immediately after it has been cooked and tossed with the sauce.

It is hard to believe that corn is not a native Italian ingredient. That's because for the past 250 years, polenta—not pasta—has been the staple of life for several northern Italian regions. Polenta, a wonderful dish that was once a poor man's staple, is now in fashion, served in delicious variations. It can be an appetizer, a first course, an entree, or a side dish. It can be served soft, straight from the pot, or cooled, sliced and baked. Polenta is almost always served next to, coated with, or topped with savory ingredients.

Rice, along with pasta and polenta, is a staple of the Italian table. Probably it came to Italy between the ninth and tenth centuries, traveling through Northern Africa, reaching Spain, and moving through Sicily into mainland Italy. The cultivation of rice in Italy took hold around the fourteenth century—basically in the north. Today, Italy is Europe's largest producer of rice.

Risotto, a rich dish, is one of the famous Italian dishes Short-grain rice is primarily used in Italian cuisine and it is essential for the making of risotto. Notably shorter and plumper than long-grain rice, it has a starchier character. Also, short-grain rice more readily releases its starches during cooking, which creates the creamy texture of a perfect risotto while the rice kernel itself remains crunchy.

The distinguishing texture of a conventionally-made risotto is said to be due to several procedures, which produce even and gradual release of the starch. This is initiated by adding the unwashed rice to the chopped onion and garlic which have been braised in olive oil to coat them with oil and prevent the overly rapid absorption of the cooking liquid. Then, release of the starches and loss of creaminess. Finally, the rice must be stirred regularly, to prevent the released starch from scorching, and to blend fat and starch.

Our recipe is altered a bit to avoid coating the rice grains with oil. The sauteing in oil actually is in effect, frying them, and we know fried foods are more difficult to digest, so are not the most beneficial. Then, too, some fried foods cause changes in the chromosomes (mutations) in the direction of cancer. We suggest instead that you follow the directions as given in the recipes that follow, and hope you enjoy our healthful and still delicious version of risotto.

Once the basic technique is understood, risotto can be flavored any way you wish. Vegetables, herbs, tofu, beans—everything's good in risotto.

"Olive oil," Sicilians say, "makes your aches and pains go away." Many people around the Mediterranean believe this and they may have a point. Olive oil is high in no-unsaturated fats. Recent studies have shown that consuming olive oil reduces the so-called bad LDL=cholesterol; thus increasing the beneficial ratio virgin cold-pressed oil as the best quality olive oil today. Also, adopt the habit of serving ripe olives very frequently.

Garlic is a must in the Italian cuisine. Not only is it a wonderful way to season your vegetarian dishes, but also an excellent natural antibiotic. Many people with hypertension have success in controlling their blood pressure with daily intake of garlic.

Cheese is very common in the Italian foods. Our health-conscious generation is becoming more concerned about the health effects of cheese. The concerns center around the following areas:

1. rich in fat.
2. high in sodium, and
3. certain cheeses may contain a variety of toxic chemicals like aflatoxins,
4. cheeses can be contaminated with a number of microorganism (salmonella, listeria e. coli, clostridium perfringens)

I am so grateful that our heavenly Father gave us an abundance in the plant kingdom, so that we can eat "for strength and not for drunkenness." Ecclesiatses 10:17, and that "He wants to satisfy our mouth with good things, so that our youth is renewed like the eagles." (Psalm 103:5)

REFERENCES:

1. Bastianich, L. Mattichio, *Lidi's Italian Table*. William Morrow and Company, Inc., NN., pp. 140, 151.

2. Caggiano, B. *Italy of Dente*. William Morrow and Co., Inc., NY, pp. 77, 149, 150, 266, 354.

3. Craig, W. J. and DeRose, D. J., Problems With Cheese. *The Journal of Health & Healing*, 17 (3): 28–30.

4. Wolfert, P. *Mediteranean Cooking*, Harper Perennial. p. 7.

PIZZA VERDURA (Vegetable Pizza) and PIZZA POCKETS*

PIZZA CRUST

1 ½ cups	whole wheat flour
½ cup	dry quick oats
1 tsp	salt
1 Tbs.	dry yeast
1 ⅔ cup	hot water
1 ½ cup	whole wheat pastry flour

Mix first four ingredients in a bowl. Add water and stir 200 times. Add the 1 ½ cup pastry flour and mix until absorbed. Let set 10 minutes. Roll out to desired thickness on a greased (or cornmeal-coated) baking sheet. Prick with fork all over and cut into circles. Bake at 400 degrees for 10 minutes, and remove.

PIZZA

Cover baked crust with Tomato Sauce, onions, broccoli, olives, bell peppers, etc., and Cheese Topping. Bake for additional 20 minutes.

---

*   Use the Pizza Crust recipe for Pizza Pockets, cutting rolled dough into circles. Spread one half of each circle with Tomato Sauce, chopped vegetables of your choice, and Cheese Topping. Fold the crust over, crimp the edges, and bake for 30 minutes at 400 degrees.

TOMATO SAUCE
(for the Pizza, Pizza Pockets, Lasagne, and Spaghetti)

15 oz.	canned tomatoes
1	chopped onion
1	chopped green pepper
½ cup	chopped celery
½ cup	sliced olives
¼ cup	corn
1 Tbs.	dried parsley flakes
1 tsp	salt
1 tsp	basil
½ tsp	Italian seasoning
2 ½ Tbs.	cornstarch dissolved in ¼ cup cold water
1 tsp	extra-virgin olive oil
3 cloves	garlic, chopped

Saute onion, pepper, and celery in a little water. Add blended tomatoes, bring to a boil, and simmer for 15 minutes. Add the remaining ingredients, stir briskly for 10 minutes to keep from lumping. Avoid cooking too long, because it will become less sweet and you may need to add a bit of honey or other sweetener.

Yield: 6 cups.

CHEESE TOPPING FOR PIZZA

½ cup	water
¼ cup	soyagen (soy milk powder)
½ tsp	salt
½ tsp	onion powder
¼ cup	oil, extra-virgin olive oil preferred
2 tsp	lemon juice
1 Tbs.	yeast flakes

Blend first four ingredients on high for 15 seconds. With blender running, slowly dribble in oil. Continue to blend for one full minute after oil is added. Stop blender and stir in lemon juice and yeast flakes.

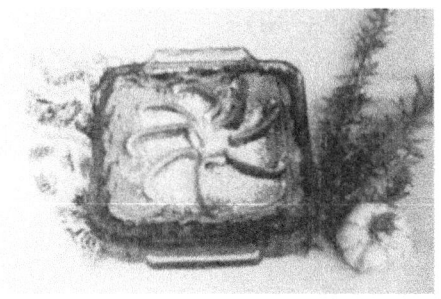

LASAGNA

12	whole wheat lasagne noodles
6 cups	Tomato Sauce
2 ½ cup	Cheese Sauce
3 Tbs.	Parmesan Cheese

Lightly coat a 9 x 13 inch lasagne pan or a casserole with Pam, and cover the bottom with 1½ cups of tomato sauce. Place uncooked noodles lengthwise, and spread some of the tomato sauce and cheese sauce on top of noodles. Repeat procedure and top with a third layer of noodles and tomato sauce. Cover and bake one hour at 350 degrees. Then uncover, drizzle with cheese sauce and garnish with sliced olives, green onions, and diced red peppers if desired. Finally, sprinkle with Parmesan Cheese. Let stand for about 15 minutes and serve. This lasagne can be assembled the day ahead and baked the next day. Baked lasagna freezes well.

Yield: 12 servings.

CHEESE SAUCE FOR LASAGNA

1 cup	sunflower seeds
1 cup	hot water
⅓ cup	yeast flakes
1½ tsp.	onion powder
⅓ cup	pimentos
⅛ tsp.	garlic powder
2 ½ Tbs.	lemon juice
1 ¼ tsp.	salt

Blend above ingredients until creamy. Then blend in additional water/cornstarch mixture as follows:

1 cup	water
1 Tbs.	cornstarch

Bring to boil, stirring frequently to prevent scorching, or cook in double boiler over boiling water, stirring frequently til thick. Remove from heat.

Yield: 2 ½ cups.

PARMESAN CHEESE (for Lasagna and Spaghetti)

¼ cup	hulled sesame seeds
½ cup	yeast flakes
2 tsp.	onion powder
½ tsp.	salt

Toast sesame seeds lightly (about 5 minutes) in 350 degree oven. Grind seeds in seed grinder or in a blender. Combine all ingredients.

SPAGHETTI WITH TOFU MEAT BALLS

1 pound	spaghetti, whole wheat, egg-free
5 quarts	water
1 tsp	salt

To serve, place plain, cooked spaghetti on a plate cover with spaghetti sauce, place tofu meat balls on top, and sprinkle with Parmesan Cheese.

Yield: 4 servings

TOFU MEAT BALLS

1 lb	extra-firm tofu, mashed
¼ cup	unfermented soy sauce
½ cup	bread crumbs
⅛ cup	chopped parsley
½ cup	chopped pecans
2 Tbs.	peanut butter
1 cup	chopped onions sauteed in water
1 tsp	yeast flakes
½ cup	chopped celery sauteed in water

Combine all ingredients and mix well. Let stand for ½ hour. Form into balls. Place onto baking pan dusted with cornmeal to prevent sticking. Bake at 350 degrees until browned (about 30 minutes)

Yield: 20 balls.

RISOTTO CON PEPPERONI
(Rice with Peppers)

1	red bell pepper, chopped
1	yellow bell pepper, chopped
½ cup	onion, chopped
2 cloves	garlic, minced
3 ¼ cups	vegetable broth
1 cup	rice
1 Tbs.	parsley, freshly chopped
¼ cup	Parmesan Cheese
1 Tbs.	olive oil (optional)

Heat the broth to boiling, add rice, cover, return to slow boil. Cover and steam over low heat for 45 minutes to 1 hour. Meanwhile, saute onion and garlic in ¼ cup water at medium burner heat, until they begin to become clear. Add peppers, stir once or twice. Add sauteed vegetables to cooked rice, stir well, then add parsley and parmesan cheese. Stir, taste, and season as desired,** and serve immediately to prevent rice from absorbing more moisture and becoming gummy.

Yield: 4 servings

**   If desired, you can add the optional olive oil at this point to enjoy its flavor and its uncooked healthful benefits.

POLENTA BREAKFAST SQUARES

5 cups	water/unsweetened pineapple juice
½ tsp	salt
2 cups	cornmeal
¾ cup	chopped or ground dates
2 tsp	vanilla
½ cup	shredded coconut

Mix all ingredients thoroughly until all lumps are dissolved. Bring the mixture to a boil and thicken while stirring. Pour it into a Pam-sprayed dish to make a ½–1 inch thick layer. Bake in the oven for one hour. Remove and chill overnight. Slice cooled polenta into squares, sprinkle them with soy milk and chopped pecans or walnuts. Place on a cookie sheet and bake in a heated oven (350 degrees) for 10 minutes. Serve hot with maple syrup, pear sauce, apple sauce, or other fruit sauce of your choice.

Yield: 12 slices

LEMON JELLO

4 cups	unsweetened pineapple juice
6 Tbs.	unflavored Emes Jel***
½ cup	honey
½ tsp	lemon extract
pinch	salt
1 Tbs.	lemon juice

Combine all ingredients and bring to boil while constantly stirring. Place in a mold and chill. Remove from the mold and serve with your choice of fruit topping.

*** We prefer Emes because this is totally animal-free, plant-based.

TIRAMISU ("PICK-ME-UP")

1 cup	cashews
2 cups	hot water
½ cup	honey
½ cup + ½ Tbs.	cornstarch
½ tsp	salt
1 pound	Mori-Nu extra-firm tofu
2 Tbs.	vanilla flavor
6 Tbs.	carob powder
2 cups	granola, soaked in carob-soy milk for 5 minutes****

Blend cashews with only one cup of hot water till creamy, and then add all remaining ingredients except granola. Place in a sauce pan and bring to a boil, stirring constantly till thick. Place a layer of granola, soaked in the carob-soy milk, in the bottom of a 9" x 9" glass pan or individual small glass dishes. Gently pour half of the above mixture over the granola, and dust it with 3 Tbs. of carob powder. Cover the carob powder with the second layer of granola and tiramisu mixture. Top with the remaining carob powder. Chill, "pick-it-up," and enjoy!

**** Carob-soy milk can be purchased in powder or packaged liquid form, or made by blending carbo powder with the soy or other nondairy milk of your choice.

We'd love to have you download our catalog of titles we publish at:

www.TEACHServices.com

or write or email us your thoughts, reactions, or criticism about this or any other book we publish at:

TEACH Services, Inc.
254 Donovan Road
Brushton, NY 12916

info@TEACHServices.com

or you may call us at:

518/358-3494